SOLUTIONS MANUAL

CLIFFORD A. SHAFFER

VIRGINIA POLYTECHNIC INSTITUTE
AND STATE UNIVERSITY

A Practical Introduction to

DATA STRUCTURES
AND
ALGORITHM ANALYSIS

CLIFFORD A. SHAFFER

PRENTICE HALL Upper Saddle River, NJ 07458

Production Editor: *Barbara Kraemer*
Buyer: *Donna Sullivan*
Publisher: *Alan Apt*
Special Projects Manager: *Barbara A. Murray*
Cover Designer: *PM Workshop Inc.*
Supplement Cover Manager: *Paul Gourhan*
Editor: *Laura Steele*

Printed in the United States of America

10 9 8 7 6 5 4 3 2

ISBN 0-13-653783-9

Prentice-Hall International (UK) Limited, *London*
Prentice-Hall of Australia Pty. Limited, *Sydney*
Prentice-Hall Canada, Inc., *Toronto*
Prentice-Hall Hispanoamericana, S.A., *Mexico*
Prentice-Hall of India Private Limited, *New Delhi*
Prentice-Hall of Japan, Inc., *Tokyo*
Simon & Schuster Asia Pte. Ltd., *Singapore*
Editora Prentice-Hall do Brasil, Ltda., *Rio de Janeiro*

Contents

Preface

Contained herein are the solutions to all exercises from the textbook *A Practical Introduction to Data Structures and Algorithm Analysis*.

For most of the problems requiring an algorithm I have given actual code. In a few cases I have presented pseudocode. Please be aware that the code presented in this manual has not actually been compiled and tested. While I believe the algorithms to be essentially correct, there may be errors in syntax as well as semantics. Most importantly, they provide a guide to the instructor as to the intended answer, rather than usable programs.

Please note that this solution manual is written for the second printing of the book. A number of the exercises from the first printing have been slightly modified for clarity, and a couple have been completely replaced. Instructors are advised, when giving an assignment, to check for differences among students' copies of the textbook and inform students of any changes to the problems.

1

Data Structures and Algorithms

1.1 This question does not have any particular right answer, provided the student keeps to the spirit of the question. Students may have trouble with the concept of "operations."

1.2 This exercise asks the student to expand on their concept of an integer representation. The answer is described by Project 4.5, where a singly-linked list is suggested. The most straightforward implementation stores each digit in its own list node, with digits stored in reverse order. Addition and multiplication are implemented by what amounts to grade-school arithmetic. For addition, simply march down in parallel through the two lists representing the operands, at each digit appending to a new list the appropriate partial sum and bringing forward a carry bit as necessary. For multiplication, combine the addition function with a new function that multiplies a single digit by an integer. Exponentiation can be done either by repeated multiplication (not really practical) or by the traditional $\Theta(\log n)$-time algorithm based on the binary representation of the exponent. Discovering this faster algorithm will be beyond the reach of most students, so should not be required.

1.3 A sample ADT for character strings might look as follows (with the normal interpretation of the function names assumed).

```
// Concatenate two strings
String strcat(String s1, String s2);

// Return the length of a string
int length(String s1);


// Extract a substring, starting at 'start',
// and of length 'length'
String extract(String s1, int start, int length);

// Get the first character
char first(String s1);

// Compare two strings: the normal C++ strcmp function. Some
// convention should be indicated for how to interpret the
// return value.  In C++, this is -1 for s1<s2; 0 for s1=s2;
// and 1 for s1>s2.
int strcmp(String s1, String s2)

// Copy a string
int strcpy(String source, String destination)
```

1.4 The answer to this question is provided by the ADT for lists given in Chapter 4.

1.5 This proposed ADT is inspired by the list ADT of Chapter 4.

```
void clear();
void insert(int);
void remove(int);
void sizeof();
bool isEmpty();
bool isInSet(int);
```

1.6 One's compliment stores the binary representation of positive numbers, and stores the binary representation of a negative number with the bits inverted. Two's compliment is the same, except that a negative number has its bits inverted and then one is added (for reasons of efficiency in hardware implementation). This representation is the physical implementation of an ADT defined by the normal arithmetic operations, declarations, and other support given by the programming language for integers.

1.7 An ADT for two-dimensional arrays might look as follows.

```
Matrix add(Matrix M1, Matrix M2);
Matrix multiply(Matrix M1, Matrix M2);
Matrix transpose(Matrix M1);
void setvalue(Matrix M1, int row, int col, int val);
int getvalue(Matrix M1, int row, int col);
List getrow(Matrix M1, int row);
```

One implementation for the sparse matrix is simply the sparse matrix implementation described in Section 12.3 Another implementation is a hash table whose search key is a concatenation of the matrix coordinates.

1.8 Every problem certainly does not have an algorithm. As discussed in Chapter 15, there are a number of reasons why this might be the case. Some problems don't have a sufficiently clear definition. Some problems, such as the halting problem, are non-computable. For some problems, such as one typically studied by artificial intelligence researchers, we simply don't know a solution.

1.9 The primitive operations are (1) adding new words to the dictionary and (2) searching the dictionary for a given word. Typically, dictionary access involves some sort of pre-processing of the word to arrive at the "root" of the word.

A twenty page document (single spaced) is likely to contain about 20,000 words. A user may be willing to wait a few seconds between individual "hits" of mis-spelled words, or perhaps up to a minute for the whole document to be processed. This means that a check for an individual word can take about 10-20 ms. Users will typically insert individual words into the dictionary interactively, so this process can take a couple of seconds. Thus, search must be much more efficient than insertion.

1.10 The user should be able to find a city based on a variety of attributes (name, location, perhaps characteristics such as population size). The user should also be able to insert and delete cities. These are the fundamental operations of any database system: search, insertion and deletion.

A reasonable database has a time constraint that will satisfy the patience of a typical user. For an insert, delete, or exact match query, a few seconds is satisfactory. If the database is meant to support range queries and mass deletions, the entire operation may be allowed to take longer, perhaps on the order of a minute. However, the time spent to process individual cities within the range must be appropriately reduced. In practice, the data representation will need to be such that it accommodates efficient processing to meet these time constraints. In particular, it may be necessary to support operations that process range queries efficiently by processing all cities in the range as a batch, rather than as a series of operations on individual cities.

1.11 A number of sorting algorithms are given in Chapter 8. Students should at least respond with answers that describe the concepts behind Insertion Sort (add the next item to a sorted list), Selection Sort (select the next smallest number from the unsorted list), and a form of divide-and-conquer such as Mergesort. Considerations of "best" should be based on time requirements. Better students will recognize that Algorithm A is better than Algorithm B in some circumstances, but not others.

1.12 The answer to this question is discussed in Chapter 8. Typical measures of cost will be number of comparisons and number of swaps. Tests should include running timings on sorted, reverse sorted, and random lists of various sizes.

1.13 The first part is easy with the hint, but the second part is rather difficult to do without a stack.

```
a) bool checkstring(string S) {
     int count = 0;
     for (int i=0; i<length(S); i++)
       if (S[i] == '(')
         count++;
       if (S[i] == ')') {
         if (count == 0) return FALSE;
         count--;
       }
   }
   if (count == 0) return TRUE;
   else return FALSE;
}
```

```
b) int checkstring(String Str) {
    Stack S;
    int count = 0;
    for (int i=0; i<length(S); i++)
      if (S[i] == '(')
        S.push(i);
      if (S[i] == ')') {
        if (S.isEmpty()) return i;
        S.pop();
      }
    }
    if (S.isEmpty()) return -1;
    else return S.pop();
}
```

1.14 Answers to this question are discussed in Section 7.2.

1.15 Answers to this question are discussed in Chapter 8.

1.16 Students at this level are likely already familiar with binary search. Thus, they should typically respond with sequential search and binary search. Binary search should be described as better since it typically needs to make fewer comparisons (and thus is likely to be much faster).

2

Mathematical Preliminaries

2.1
```
long ifact(int n) {// n <= 12 so n! fits in long int variable
   long fact = 1;
   assert((n >= 0) && (n <= 12)); // Base case: legal bounds
   for (int i=1; i<= n; i++)
      fact = fact * i;
   return fact;
}
```

2.2
```
void rpermute(int *array, int n) {
   swap(array[n-1], array[Random(n)]);
   rpermute(int *array, n-1);
}
```

2.3 Fibr is so much slower than Fibi because Fibr re-computes the bulk of the series twice to get the two values to add. What is much worse, the recursive calls to compute the subexpressions also re-compute the bulk of the series, and do so recursively. The result is an exponential explosion. In contrast, Fibi computes each value in the series exactly once, and so its running time is proportional to n.

2.4
```
// Array curr[i] indicates the current position of ring i.
void GenTOH(int n, POLE goal, POLE t1, POLE t2, POLE* curr) {
   if (curr[n] == goal) // Only need to get top n-1 rings set up
      GenTOH(n-1, goal, t1, t2, curr);
   else {
      if (curr[n] == t1) swap(t1, t2); // Get the names right
      // Now, ring n is on pole t2.  Put others on t1.
      GenTOH(n-1, t1, goal, t2, curr);
      move(t2, goal);
      GenTOH(n-1, goal, t1, t2, curr); // Now move n-1 rings back
   }
}
```

2.5 Proof: Assume that there is a largest prime number. Call it P_n, the nth largest prime number, and label all of the primes in order $P_1 = 2$, $P_2 = 3$, and so on. Now, consider the number C formed by multiplying all of the n prime numbers together. The value $C + 1$ is not divisible by any of the n prime numbers. $C + 1$ is a prime number larger than P_n, a contradiction. Thus, we conclude that there is no largest prime number. □

2.6 Note: This problem is harder than most sophomore level students can handle.

Proof: The proof is by contradiction. Assume that $\sqrt{2}$ is rational. By definition, there exist integers p and q such that

$$\sqrt{2} = \frac{p}{q},$$

where p and q have no common factors (that is, the fraction p/q is in lowest terms). By squaring both sides and doing some simple algebraic manipulation, we get

$$2 = \frac{p^2}{q^2}$$
$$2q^2 = p^2$$

Since p^2 must be even, p must be even. Thus,

$$2q^2 = 4(\frac{p}{2})^2$$
$$q^2 = 2(\frac{p}{2})^2$$

This implies that q^2 is also even. Thus, p and q are both even, which contradicts the requirement that p and q have no common factors. Thus, $\sqrt{2}$ must be irrational. □

2.7 The leftmost summation sums the integers from 1 to n. The second summation merely reverses this order, summing the numbers from $n - 1 + 1 = n$ down to $n - n + 1 = 1$. The third summation has a variable substitution of $i - 1$ for i, with a corresponding substitution in the summation bounds. Thus, it is also the summation of $n - 0 = n$ to $n - (n - 1) = 1$.

2.8 Proof:

(a) **Base case.** For $n = 1$, $1^2 = [2(1)^3 + 3(1)^2 + 1]/6 = 1$. Thus, the formula is correct for the base case.

(b) Induction Hypothesis.

$$\sum_{i=1}^{n-1} i^2 = \frac{2(n-1)^3 + 3(n-1)^2 + (n-1)}{6}.$$

(c) Induction Step.

$$\begin{aligned}
\sum_{i=1}^{n} i^2 &= \sum_{i=1}^{n-1} i^2 + n^2 \\
&= \frac{2(n-1)^3 + 3(n-1)^2 + (n-1)}{6} + n^2 \\
&= \frac{2n^3 - 6n^2 + 6n - 2 + 3n^2 - 6n + 3 + n - 1}{6} + n^2 \\
&= \frac{2n^3 + 3n^2 + n}{6}.
\end{aligned}$$

Thus, the theorem is proved by mathematical induction.   □

2.9 Proof:

(a) Base case. For $n = 1$, $1/2 = 1 - 1/2 = 1/2$. Thus, the formula is correct for the base case.

(b) Induction Hypothesis.

$$\sum_{i=1}^{n-1} \frac{1}{2^i} = 1 - \frac{1}{2^{n-1}}.$$

(c) Induction Step.

$$\begin{aligned}
\sum_{i=1}^{n} \frac{1}{2^i} &= \sum_{i=1}^{n-1} \frac{1}{2^i} + \frac{1}{2^n} \\
&= 1 - \frac{1}{2^{n-1}} + \frac{1}{2^n} \\
&= 1 - \frac{1}{2^n}.
\end{aligned}$$

Thus, the theorem is proved by mathematical induction.   □

2.10 Proof:

(a) Base case. For $n = 0$, $2^0 = 2^1 - 1 = 1$. Thus, the formula is correct for the base case.

(b) **Induction Hypothesis.**

$$\sum_{i=0}^{n-1} 2^i = 2^n - 1.$$

(c) Induction Step.

$$\begin{aligned}
\sum_{i=0}^{n} 2^i &= \sum_{i=0}^{n-1} 2^i + 2^n \\
&= 2^n - 1 + 2^n \\
&= 2^{n+1} - 1.
\end{aligned}$$

Thus, the theorem is proved by mathematical induction. □

2.11 Theorem 2.1 $\sum_{i=1}^{n}(2i) = n^2 + n$.

(a) **Proof:** We know from Example 2.3 that the sum of the first n odd numbers is n^2. The ith even number is simply one greater than the ith odd number. Since we are adding n such numbers, the sum must be n greater, or $n^2 + n$. □

(b) **Proof:** The base case of $n = 1$ yields $2 = 1^2 + 1$, which is true. The induction hypothesis is

$$\sum_{i=1}^{n-1} 2i = (n-1)^2 + (n-1).$$

We now use the induction hypothesis to show that the theorem holds true for n. The sum of the first n even numbers is simply the sum of the first $n-1$ even numbers plus the nth even number.

$$\begin{aligned}
\sum_{i=1}^{n} 2i &= \left(\sum_{i=1}^{n-1} 2i\right) + 2n \\
&= (n-1)^2 + (n-1) + 2n \\
&= (n^2 - 2n + 1) + (n-1) + 2n \\
&= n^2 - n + 2n \\
&= n^2 + n.
\end{aligned}$$

Thus, by mathematical induction, $\sum_{i=1}^{n} 2i = n^2 + n$. □

2.12 Proof:

   (a) Base case. For $n = 1$, $Fib(1) = 1 < \frac{5}{3}$. Thus, the formula is correct for the base case.

   (b) Induction Hypothesis.

$$Fib(n-1) < (\frac{5}{3})^{n-1}.$$

   (c) Induction Step. $Fib(n) = Fib(n-1) + Fib(n-2)$ and, by the Induction Hypothesis, $Fib(n-1) < \frac{5}{3}^{n-1}$ and $Fib(n-2) < \frac{5}{3}^{n-2}$. So,

$$
\begin{aligned}
Fib(n) &< \frac{5}{3}^{n-1} + \frac{5}{3}^{n-2} \\
&< \frac{5}{3}(\frac{5}{3}^{n-2}) + \frac{5}{3}^{n-2} \\
&= \frac{8}{3}(\frac{5}{3}^{n-2}) \\
&< \frac{5^2}{3}(\frac{5}{3}^{n-2}) \\
&= \frac{5}{3}^{n}.
\end{aligned}
$$

Thus, the theorem is proved by mathematical induction.   □

2.13 Proof:

   (a) Base case. For $n = 1$, $1^3 = \frac{1^2(1+1)^2}{4} = 1$. Thus, the formula is correct for the base case.

   (b) Induction Hypothesis.

$$\sum_{i=0}^{n-1} i^3 = \frac{(n-1)^2 n^2}{4}.$$

   (c) Induction Step.

$$
\begin{aligned}
\sum_{i=0}^{n} i^3 &= \frac{(n-1)^2 n^2}{4} + n^3 \\
&= \frac{n^4 - 2n^3 + n^2}{4} + n^3 \\
&= \frac{n^4 + 2n^3 + n^2}{4}
\end{aligned}
$$

$$= \frac{n^2(n^2 + 2n + 2)}{4}$$

$$= \frac{n^2(n + 1)^2}{4}$$

Thus, the theorem is proved by mathematical induction. □

2.14 **(a)** **Proof**: By contradiction. Assume that the theorem is false. Then, each pigeonhole contains at most 1 pigeon. Since there are n holes, there is room for only n pigeons. This contradicts the fact that a total of $n+1$ pigeons are within the n holes. Thus, the theorem must be correct. □

(b) **Proof**:

i. **Base case.** For one pigeon hole and two pigeons, there must be two pigeons in the hole.

ii. **Induction Hypothesis.** For n pigeons in $n-1$ holes, some hole must contain at least two pigeons.

iii. Induction Step. Consider the case where $n + 1$ pigeons are in n holes. Eliminate one hole at random. If it contains one pigeon, eliminate it as well, and by the induction hypothesis some other hole must contain at least two pigeons. If it contains no pigeons, then again by the induction hypothesis some other hole must contain at least two pigeons (with an extra pigeon yet to be placed). If it contains more than one pigeon, then it fits the requirements of the theorem directly.

□

2.15 **(a)** The probability is 0.5 for each choice.

(b) The average number of "1" bits is $n/2$, since each position has 0.5 probability of being "1."

(c) The leftmost "1" will be the leftmost bit (call it position 0) with probability 0.5; in position 1 with probability 0.25, and so on. The number of positions we must examine is 1 in the case where the leftmost "1" is in position 0; 2 when it is in position 1, and so on. Thus, the expected cost is the value of the summation

$$\sum_{i=1}^{n} \frac{i}{2^i}.$$

The closed form for this summation is $2 - \frac{n+2}{2^n}$, or just less than two. Thus, we expect to visit on average just less than two positions. (Students at this point will probably not be able to solve this summation, and it is not given in the book.)

2.16 There are typically two ways to approach this problem. One is to estimate the volume directly. The second is to generate volume as a function of weight. This is especially easy if using the metric system, assuming that the human body is roughly the density of water. So a 50 Kilo person has a volume slightly less than 50 liters; a 160 pound person has a volume slightly less than 20 gallons.

2.17 **(a)** Image representations vary considerably, so the answer will vary as a result. One example answer is: Consider VGA standard size, full-color (24 bit) images, which is $3 \times 640 \times 480$, or just less than 1 Mbyte per image. The full database requires some 30-35 CDs.

(b) Since we needed 30-35 CDs before, compressing by a factor of 10 is not sufficient to get the database onto one CD.

[Note that if the student picked a smaller format, such as estimating the size of a "typical" gif image, the result might well fit onto a single CD.]

2.18 (I saw this problem in John Bentley's *Programming Pearls*.) The Mississippi river at its mouth is about 1/4 mile wide and 100 feet (1/50 mile) deep, with a flow of around 15 miles/hour = 360 mile/day. Thus, the flow is about 2 cubic miles/day. Bentley also suggests calculating based on rainfall as a second check on the estimate.

2.19 Note that the student should NOT be providing answers that look like they were done using a calculator. This is supposed to be an exercise in estimation!

The amount of the mortgage is irrelevant, since this is a question about rates. However, to give some numbers to estimate from, pick a $100,000 mortgage. The up-front charge would be $1,000, and the savings would be 1/4% each payment over the life of the mortgage. Given a 15 year mortgage, the difference in interest charges per month will on average be half the charge for the full amount of the mortgage (in the first month, you get full charge; in the last month nearly no charge). So, 8% of $100,000 is $8,000, while 7 3/4% is $7,750 (for the first year). This will require a payback period of about 4 years. If they money had been invested, then in 5 years the investment would be worth about $1300, so the payback would be close to 5 1/2 years.

2.20 Disk drive seek time is around 10 milliseconds (in late 1996). RAM memory requires around 50 nanoseconds – much less than a microsecond. Given that there are about 30 million seconds in a year, a machine capable of executing at 30-40 MIPS would execute about 1 million billion (10^{15}) instructions in a year.

2.21 Typical books have around 500 pages/inch of thickness, so one million pages requires 2000 inches or 150-200 feet of bookshelf. This would be in excess of 50 typical shelves, or 10-20 bookshelves. It is within the realm of possibility that an individual home has this many books, but it is rather unusual.

2.22 A typical page has around 400 words (best way to derive this is to estimate the number of words/line and lines/page), and the book has around 500 pages, so the total is around 200,000 words.

2.23 An hour has 3600 seconds, so one million seconds is a bit less than 300 hours. A good estimater will notice that 3600 is about 10% greater than 3333, so the actual number of hours is about 10% less than 300, or close to 270. (The real value is just under 278). Of course, this is just over 11 days.

2.24 Well over 100,000, depending on what you wish to count. The real question is what technique the student uses.

2.25 **(a)** The time required is 1 minute for the first mile, then 60/59 minutes for the second mile, and so on until the last mile requires $60/1 = 60$ minutes. The result is the following summation.

$$\sum_{i=1}^{60} 60/i = 60 \sum_{i=1}^{60} 1/i = 60\mathcal{H}_{60}.$$

(b) This is actually quite easy. The man will never reach his destination, since his speed approaches zero as he approaches the end of the journey.

3

Algorithm Analysis

3.1 $5n \log n$ is most efficient for $n = 1$.
2^n is most efficient when $2 \leq n \leq 4$.
$10n$ is most efficient for all $n > 5$.

3.2   Both $\log_3 n$ and $\log_2 n$ will have value 0 when $n = 1$.
Otherwise, 2 is the most efficient expression for all $n > 1$.

3.3

$$2 \quad log_3 n \quad \log_2 n \quad 20n \quad n^{2/3} \quad 4n^2 \quad 3^n \quad n!.$$

3.4 **(a)** $n + 6$ inputs (an additive amount, independent of n).

(b) $8n$ inputs (a multiplicative factor).

(c) $64n$ inputs.

3.5 $100n$.
$10n$.
About $4.6n$ (actually, $\sqrt[3]{100n}$).
$n + 6$.

3.6 Other values for n_0 and c are possible than what is given here.

(a) The upper bound is $O(n)$ for $n_0 > 0$ and $c = c_1$. The lower bound is $\Omega(n)$ for $n_0 > 0$ and $c = c_1$.

(b) The upper bound is $O(n^3)$ for $n_0 > c_3$ and $c = c_2 + 1$. The lower bound is $\Omega(n^3)$ for $n_0 > c_3$ and $c = c_2$.

(c) The upper bound is $O(n \log n)$ for $n_0 > c_5$ and $c = c_4 + 1$. The lower bound is $\Omega(n \log n)$ for $n_0 > c_5$ and $c = c_4$.

(d) The upper bound is $O(2^n)$ for $n_0 > c_7 100$ and $c = c_6 + 1$. The lower bound is $\Omega(2^n)$ for $n_0 > c_7 100$ and $c = c_6$. (100 is used for convenience to insure that $2^n > n^6$)

3.7 Yes. Each deterministic algorithm, on a given input, has a specific running time. Its upper and lower bound are the same – exactly this time. Note that the question asks for the EXISTENCE of such a thing, not our ability to determine it.

3.8 (a) $f(n) = \Theta(g(n))$ since $\log n^2 = 2 \log n$.

(b) $f(n)$ is in $\Omega(g(n))$ since $\sqrt{n}$ grows faster than $\log n^c$ for any c.

(c) $f(n)$ is in $O(g(n))$ since $\log n$ grows faster than $\log^2 n$.

(d) $f(n)$ is in $\Omega(g(n))$ since n grows faster than $\log^2 n$.

(e) $f(n)$ is in $\Omega(g(n))$ since $n \log n$ grows faster than $\log n$.

(f) $f(n) = \Theta(g(n))$ since $\log 10$ and 10 are both constants.

(g) $f(n)$ is in $\Omega(g(n))$ since 2^n grows faster than $10n^2$.

(h) $f(n)$ is in $O(g(n))$ since 3^n grows faster than 2^n.

3.9 (a) This fragment is $\Theta(1)$.

(b) This fragment is $\Theta(n)$ since the outer loop is executed a constant number of times.

(c) This fragment is $\Theta(n^2)$ since the loop is executed n^2 times.

(d) This fragment is $\Theta(n^2 \log n)$ since the outer for loop costs $n \log n$ for each execution, and is executed n times. The inner loop is dominated by the call to sort.

(e) For each execution of the outer loop, the inner loop is generated a "random" number of times. However, since the values in the array are a permutation of the values from 0 to $n-1$, we know that the inner loop will be run i times for each value of i from 1 to n. Thus, the total cost is $\sum_{i=1}^{n} i = \Theta(n^2)$.

(f) One branch of the if statement requires $\Theta(n)$ time, while the other requires constant time. By the rule for if statements, the bound is the greater cost, yielding $\Theta(n)$ time.

3.10 (a)

$$
\begin{aligned}
n! &= n \times (n-1) \times \cdots \times \frac{n}{2} \times \left(\frac{n}{2} - 1\right) \times \cdots \times 2 \times 1 \\
&\geq \frac{n}{2} \times \frac{n}{2} \times \cdots \times \frac{n}{2} \times 1 \times \cdots \times 1 \times 1 \\
&= \left(\frac{n}{2}\right)^{n/2}
\end{aligned}
$$

Therefore

$$
\lg n! \geq \lg \left(\frac{n}{2}\right)^{\frac{n}{2}} \geq \frac{1}{2}(n \lg n - n).
$$

(b) This part is easy, since clearly

$$1 \cdot 2 \cdot 3 \cdots n < n \cdot n \cdot n \cdots n,$$

so $n! < n^n$ yielding $\log n! < n \log n$.

3.11 The best lower bound I know is $\Omega(\log n)$, since a value cannot be reduced more quickly than by repeated division by 2. There is no known upper bound, since it is unknown if this algorithm always terminates.

3.12 Yes. When we specify an upper or lower bound, that merely states our knowledge of the situation. If they do not meet, that merely means that we don't KNOW more about the problem. When we understand the problem completely, the bounds will meet. But, that does NOT mean that we can actually determine the optimal algorithm, or the true lower bound, for every problem.

3.13
```
int newbin(int K, int* array, int left, int right) {
  // Return position of element in array (if any) with value K
  int l = left-1;
  int r = right+1;    // l and r are beyond bounds of array
  while (l+1 != r) {   // Stop when l and r meet
    int i = (l+r)/2;   // Look at middle of remaining subarray
    if (K <= array[i]) r = i;   // In left half
    if (K > array[i]) l = i;    // In right half
  }
  if (r > right) return ERROR;  // K not in array
  if (array[r] != K) return ERROR; // K not in array
  else return r;      // r at value K
}
```

3.14
```
int newbin(int K, int* array, int left, int right) {
  // Return position of element in array (if any) with value K
  int l = left-1;
  int r = right+1;    // l and r are beyond bounds of array
  while (l+1 != r) {   // Stop when l and r meet
    int i = (l+r)/2;   // Look at middle of remaining subarray
    if (K < array[i]) r = i;    // In left half
    if (K == array[i]) return i; // Found it
    if (K > array[i]) l = i;    // In right half
  }
  // Search value not in array
  if (l < left) return ERROR;  // No value less than K
  else  return l;              // l at first value less than K
}
```

3.15 Here is a description for a simple $\Theta(n^2)$ algorithm.

```
boolean Corner(int n, int m, Piece P1, Piece** array) {
  for (int i=0; i<n; i++)
    for (int j=0; j<n; j++) {
      if (compare(P1, array[i][j], LEFT)) return FALSE;
      if (compare(P1, array[i][j], BOTTOM)) return FALSE;
    }
  return TRUE;
}


void jigsaw(int n, int m, Piece** array) {
\\ First, find the lower left piece by checking each piece
\\ against the others to reject pieces until one is found
\\ that has no bottom or left connection.
for (i=0; i<n; i++)
  for (j=0; j<m; j++)
    if (Corner(n, m, array[i][j], array)) { // Found it.
      SWAP(array[i][j], array[0][0]); // Swap two pieces
      break;
    }
\\ Now, fill in row by row, column by column.
for (i=0; i<n; i++)
  for (j=0; j<m; j++) {
    if (j==0) { // First in row
      if (i!=0) { // Don't repeat corner piece
        for (ii=0; ii<n; ii++)
          for (jj=0; jj<m; jj++)
            if (compare(array[i][j], array[ii][jj], TOP)) {
              tempr = ii;
              tempc = jj;
            }
        SWAP(array[i][j], array[tempr][tempc]);
      }}
    else {
      for (ii=0; ii<n; ii++)
        for (jj=0; jj<m; jj++)
          if (compare(array[i][j], array[ii][jj], RIGHT))
            { tempr = ii;  tempc = jj; }
      SWAP(array[i][j], array[tempr][tempc]);
    }
  }
}
```

Finding the corner takes $O(n^2m^2)$ time, which is the number of pieces squared. Filling in the rest of the pieces also takes $O(n^2m^2)$ time, the number of pieces squared. Thus, the entire algorithm takes $O(n^2m^2)$ time.

3.16 If an algorithm is $\Theta(f(n))$ in the average case, then by definition it is $\Omega(f(n))$ in the average case. Since the average case cost for an instance of the problem requires at lest $cf(n)$ time for some constant c, at least one instance requires at least as much as the average cost (this is an example of applying the Pigeonhole Principle). Thus, at least one instance costs at least $cf(n)$, and so this means at least one instance (the worst case) is $\Omega(f(n))$.

4

Lists, Stacks, and Queues

4.1 Call the list in question L1.

```
L1.setFirst();
L1.next();
L1.next();
val = L1.remove();
```

4.2 The space required by the array-based list implementation is fixed. It must be at least n spaces to hold n elements, for a lower bound of $\Omega(n)$. However, the actual number of elements in the array (n) can be arbitrarily small compared to the size of the list array.

4.3 **(a)** (10, 20, 15) with 15 being the current element.

(b) (39, 12, 10, 20, 15) with 12 being the current element.

4.4 `list L1(20);`
`L1.append(2);`
`L1.append(23);`
`L1.append(15);`
`L1.append(5);`
`L1.append(9);`

4.5 D is number of elements; E is in bytes; P is in bytes; and n is number of elements. Setting number of elements as e and number of bytes as b, the equation has form

$$e > eb/(b+b) = eb/b = e$$

for a comparison of $e > e$ which is correct.

4.6 Since $E = 8$, $P = 4$, and $D = 20$, the break-even point occurs when

$$n = (20)(8)/(4 + 8) = 13\frac{1}{3}.$$

So, the linked list is more efficient when there are 13 or fewer elements stored.

4.7 The following members are modified.

```
list::list(const int sz) {      // Constructor -- Ignore sz
  head = tail = curr = new link;  // Create header node
  head->next = head;
}

void list::clear() {            // Remove all ELEMs from list
  while (head->next != NULL) { // Return nodes to free store
    curr = head->next;          //    (keep header node)
    head->next = curr->next;
    delete curr;
  }
  tail = curr = head->next = head;          // Reinitialize
}

// Insert ELEM at current position
void list::insert(const ELEM& item) {
  assert(curr != NULL);         // Must be pointing to list ELEM
  curr->next = new link(item, curr->next);
  if (tail->next != head) tail = tail->next;
}

void list::append(const ELEM& item) // Insert ELEM at tail
  { tail = tail->next = new link(item, head); }

void list::next()                   // Move curr to next position
  { curr = curr->next; }

void list::prev() {                 // Move curr to prev position
  link* temp = curr;
  while (temp->next!=curr) temp=temp->next;
  curr = temp;
}

bool list::isEmpty() const          // Return TRUE if empty list
  { return head->next == head; }
```

```
bool list::isInList() const         // TRUE if curr within list
  { return (curr != NULL) && (curr->next != head); }

bool list::find(const ELEM& val) {  // Find val (start at curr)
  link* temp = curr;
  while (curr->next != temp)
    if (curr->next->element == val) return TRUE;
    else curr = curr->next;
  return FALSE;                     // Not found
}
```

4.8 The answer is rather similar to that of Question 4.7.

4.9
```
\\ Interchange the order of the current and next elements.
void switch(LIST L1) {
  ELEM temp = L1.remove();
  L1.next();
  L1.insert(temp);
}
```

4.10
```
void list::reverse() { // Reverse the contents of the list
  if(head->next == NULL) return;
  link* temp1 = head->next;
  link* temp2 = temp1->next;
  while (temp2 != NULL) {
    link* temp3 = temp2->next;
    temp2->next = temp1;
    temp1 = temp2;
    temp2 = temp3;
  }
  head->next = temp1;
}
```

4.11 We need only modify push and pop, as follows.

```
void push(const ELEM& item) {   // Push ELEM onto stack
  assert(top + length(item) < size);
  for (int i=0; i<length(item) i++)
    listarray[top++] = item[i];
  listarray[top++] = length(item);
}

ELEM pop(ELEM& item) {          // Pop ELEM from top of stack
  assert(!isEmpty());
  int length = listarray[top--];
```

```
      for (int i=1; i<=length; i++)
        item[length - i] = listarray[top--];
      return item;
    }
```

4.12 Most member functions get a new parameter to indicate which stack
is accessed.

```
class Stack2 {                      // Array based stack class
private:
  int size;                         // Maximum size of stack
  int top1, top2;                   // Index for top ELEMs (two)
  ELEM *listarray;                  // Array holding stack ELEM's

public:
  Stack(const int sz =LIST_SIZE)    // Constructor: initialize
    { size = sz; top1 = 0; top2 = sz-1;
      listarray = new ELEM[sz]; }
  ~Stack()                          // Destructor: return array space
    { delete [] listarray; }
  void clear(int st) {              // Remove all ELEM's from stack
    if (st == 1) top1 = 0;
    else top2 = size-1;
  }
  void push(int st, const ELEM& item) { // Push ELEM onto stack
    assert(top1+1 < top2); // Not full
    if (st == 1) listarray[top1++] = item;
    else listarray[top2--] = item;
  }
  ELEM pop(int st) {                // Pop ELEM from top of stack
    assert(!isEmpty(st));
    if (st == 1) return listarray[--top1];
    else return listarray[++top2];
  }
  ELEM topValue(int st) const {  // Return value of top ELEM
    assert(!isEmpty(st));
    if (st == 1) return listarray[top1-1];
    else return listarray[top2+1];
  }
  bool isEmpty(int st) const { // Return TRUE if stack is empty
    if (st == 1) return top1 == 0;
    else return top2 == n-1;
  }
};
```

4.13 The stack stores records containing an operation (TOH or MOVE), number of disks, start, goal and temp poles. In the code, Push and Pop operations should be interpreted as pushing and popping this series of values.

```
void StackTOH(n, start, goal, temp) {
  Stack S;
  S.Push(TOH, n, start, goal, temp); // Initial configuration
  while (!S.isEmpty()) {
    S.Pop(OP, n, start, goal, temp); // Pop off the record into
                                     // these fields
   if (OP == MOVE)
      move(start, goal);  // Just like in recursive form
    else if (n > 0) { // Imitate the three statements in TOH
                   //   solution (in reverse)
      S.Push(TOH, n-1, temp, goal, start); // 2nd operation
      S.Push(MOVE, n, start, goal, temp);  // A move to do
      S.Push(TOH, n-1, start, temp, goal); // 1st operation
    }
  }
}
```

4.14 On my UNIX machine, both int and pointers require 4 bytes. Thus, the break-even point occurs when the array is half full.

4.15
```
class Queue {                    // Array based queue class
private:
  int size;                      // Maximum size of queue
  int front;                     // Index prior to front item
  int rear;                      // Index of rear item
  ELEM *listarray;               // Array holding the list ELEM's
  bool emptyflag;                // TRUE iff queue is empty
public:
  Queue(const int sz =LIST_SIZE)    // Constructor
    { // Make list array one position larger for empty slot
      size = sz+1;  front = rear = 0;
      listarray = new ELEM[size];
      emptyflag = TRUE; }
  ~Queue() { delete [] listarray; } // Destructor
  void clear() { front = rear; emptyflag = TRUE} // Clear queue
  void enqueue(const ELEM&);        // Enqueue ELEM at rear
  ELEM dequeue();                   // Dequeue ELEM from front
  ELEM firstValue() const           // Get value of front ELEM
    { assert(!isEmpty()); return listarray[(front+1) % size]; }
```

```
      bool isEmpty() const              // TRUE if queue is empty
        { return emptyflag; }
    };

    // Enqueue ELEM at rear of queue
    void Queue::enqueue(const ELEM& item) {
      assert(((rear) % size) != front); // Queue must not be full
      rear = (rear+1) % size;         // Increment rear (in circle)
      listarray[rear] = item;
      emptyflag = FALSE;
    }

    ELEM Queue::dequeue() {   // Dequeue ELEM from front of queue
      assert(!isEmpty());     // There must be something to dequeue
      front = (front+1) % size; // Increment front
      if (front == rear) emptyflag == TRUE;
      return listarray[front];  // Return value
    }
```

4.16
```
    typedef ELEM char;

    bool palin() {
      Stack S;
      Queue Q;

      while ((c = getc()) != ENDOFSTRING) {
        S.push(c);
        Q.enqueue(c);
      }
      while (!S.isEmpty()) {
        if (S.top() != Q.front()) return FALSE;
        char dum = S.pop();
        dum = Q.dequeue();
      }
      return TRUE;
    }
```

4.17
```
    void reverse(Queue& Q, Stack& S) {
      ELEM X;
      while (!Q.isEmpty()) {
        X = Q.dequeue();
        S.push(X);
      }
      while (!S.isEmpty()) {
        X = S.pop();
```

```
      Q.enqueue(X);
   }
}
```

4.18 Some additional access capability must be added. One approach is to add more pointers to the linked list structure. By granting direct access half way in, from there to the quarter lists, etc., it is possible to gain $O(\log n)$ insert and search times. This concept will lead to the Skip List of Chapter 13. Alternatively, we can adopt the tree concept, discussed in Chapter 5.

4.19 (a) `typedef ELEM char;`

```
bool balance(char* string) {
  Stack S;
  int pos = 0;
  while (string[pos] != NULL) {
    if (string[pos++] == '(')
      S.push('(');
    else if (string[pos++] == ')')
      if (S.isEmpty()) return FALSE;
      else S.pop();
  }
  if (S.isEmpty()) return TRUE;
  else return FALSE;
}
```

(b) `typedef ELEM int;`

```
int balance(char* string) {
  Stack S;
  int pos = 0;
  while (string[pos] != NULL) {
    if (string[pos++] == '(')
      S.push(pos);
    else if (string[pos++] == ')')
      if (S.isEmpty()) return pos;
      else S.pop();
  }
  if (S.isEmpty()) return -1;
  else return S.pop();
}
```

5

Binary Trees

5.1 Consider a non-full binary tree. By definition, this tree must have some internal node X with only one non-empty child. If we modify the tree to remove X, replacing it with its child, the modified tree will have a higher fraction of non-empty nodes since one non-empty node and one empty node have been removed.

5.2 Use as the base case the tree of one leaf node. Here the number of degree 2 nodes is 0, and the number of leaves is 1. Thus, the theorem holds.

For the induction hypothesis, assume the theorem is true for any tree with n nodes of degree 2.

For the induction step, add a new (leaf) node to any tree with n nodes of degree 2. If the new node is added to a parent of degree 1, then 1 new leaf is added and one new node of degree 2 is created, so the theorem holds. Alternatively, if the new node is added to a parent of degree 0 (a leaf node), then no new node of degree 2 is added, but the number of leaf nodes stays the same since the new node is a leaf, but its parent is no longer a leaf. Thus, the theorem still holds. By mathematical induction, the theorem is correct.

5.3 (a)
```
void inorder(BinNode* rt)  // rt is the root of a subtree
{
    if (rt == NULL) return;   // Empty subtree
    inorder(rt->leftchild());
    visit(rt);  // visit performs whatever action is desired
    inorder(rt->rightchild());
}
```

(b)
```
void postorder(BinNode* rt)   // rt is the root of a subtree
{
    if (rt == NULL) return;   // Empty subtree
    postorder(rt->leftchild());
    postorder(rt->rightchild());
    visit(rt);   // visit performs whatever action is desired
}
```

5.4 **(a)** Since every node stores 4 bytes of data and 12 bytes of pointers, the overhead fraction is $12/16 = 75\%$.

(b) Since every node stores 16 bytes of data and 8 bytes of pointers, the overhead fraction is $8/24 \approx 33\%$.

(c) Leaf nodes store 8 bytes of data and 4 bytes of pointers; internal nodes store 8 bytes of data and 12 bytes of pointers. Since the nodes have different sizes, the total space needed for internal nodes is not the same as for leaf nodes. Students must be careful to do the calculation correctly, taking the weighting into account. The correct formula looks as follows, given that there are x internal nodes and x leaf nodes.

$$\frac{4x + 12x}{12x + 20x} = 16/32 = 50\%.$$

5.5 The key is to search both subtrees, as necessary.

```
bool search(BinNode* rt, int K) {
    if (rt == NULL) return FALSE;
    if (rt->value() == K) return TRUE;
    if (search(rt->rightchild())) return TRUE;
    return search(rt->leftchild());
}
```

5.6 The key is to use a queue to store subtrees to be processed.

```
typedef ELEM BinNode*;   // Store a queue of node pointers
void level(BinNode* rt) {
    Queue Q;
    Q.enqueue(rt);
    while(!Q.isEmpty()) {
        BinNode* temp = Q.dequeue();
        if(temp != NULL) {
            Print(temp);
            Q.enqueue(temp->leftchild());
            Q.enqueue(temp->rightchild());
}}}
```

5.7 Base Case: For the tree of one leaf node, $I = 0$, $E = 0$, $n = 0$, so the theorem holds.

Induction Hypothesis: The theorem holds for the full binary tree containing n internal nodes.

Induction Step: Take an arbitrary leaf node, and add two children to it. Call the depth of this node d. The two new leaf nodes are at depth $d + 1$. I has increased by a value of d. E has increased by a value of $2(d + 1) - d = d + 2$ since two new leaf nodes are added and one removed (to become the internal node). n has increased by one. Thus, if before the addition we had $E = I + 2n$ (by the induction hypothesis), then after the addition we have $E + d + 2 = I + d + 2(n + 1)$ which is correct. Thus, by the principle of mathematical induction, the theorem is correct.

5.8 Here are the final codes, rather than a picture.

l	00
h	010
i	011
e	1000
f	1001
j	101
d	11000
a	1100100
b	1100101
c	110011
g	1101
k	111

The average code length is 3.23445

5.9 The set of sixteen characters with equal weight will create a Huffman coding tree that is complete with 16 leaf nodes all at depth 4. Thus, the average code length will be 4 bits. This is identical to the fixed length code. Thus, in this situation, the Huffman coding tree saves no space (and costs no space).

5.10 (a) By the prefix property, there can be no character with codes 0, 00, or 001x where "x" stands for any binary string.

(b) There must be at least one code with each form 1x, 01x, 000x where "x" could be any binary string (including the empty string).

5.11 **(a)** Q and Z are at level 5, so any string of length n containing only Q's and Z's requires $5n$ bits.

(b) O and E are at level 2, so any string of length n containing only O's and E's requires $2n$ bits.

(c) The weighted average is

$$\frac{5 * 5 + 10 * 4 + 35 * 3 + 50 * 2}{100} = 2.7$$

bits per character

5.12 The minimum number of elements is contained in the heap with a single node at depth $h - 1$, for a total of 2^{h-1} nodes.

The maximum number of elements is contained in the heap that has completely filled up level $h - 1$, for a total of $2^h - 1$ nodes.

5.13 The largest element could be at any leaf node.

5.14 This is a straightforward modification. We assume some appropriate syntax for inserting the record containing a tree: The heap insert routine must look at the weight of the tree.

```
// Build Huffman tree from list tmplist
HuffTree* build_tree(list& tmplist) {
  HuffTree *temp1, *temp2, *temp3;
  heap h;

  // Build heap
  tmplist.setFirst();
  while(tmplist.isInList()) {
    temp1 = tmplist.remove();
    h.insert(temp1);
  }
  // Now, build tree
  while(h.size() > 1) {
    temp1 = h.removemin();
    temp2 = h.removemin();
    temp3 = new HuffTree(tempnode, temp1, temp2);
    h.insert(temp3);
  }
  return h.removemin(); // Return the tree
}
```

5.15 If equal valued nodes were allowed to appear in either subtree, then during a search for all nodes of a given value, whenever we encounter a node of that value the search would be required to search in both directions.

5.16 This tree will be identical to the tree of Figure 5.20(a), except that a node with value 5 will be added as the right child of the node with value 2.

5.17 This tree will be identical to the tree of Figure 5.20(b), except that the value 24 replaces the value 7, and the leaf node that originally contained 24 is removed from the tree.

5.18
```
int COUNT(BinNode* root, int K) {
    if (root == NULL) return 0;
    if (root->value() > K)
      return COUNT(root->leftchild(), K);
    else
      return COUNT(root->leftchild(), K) +
             COUNT(root->rightchild(), K) + 1;
```

5.19
```
void PRINT_RANGE(BinNode* root, int low, int high) {
    if (root == NULL) return;
    if (root->value() > high)
      PRINT_RANGE(root->leftchild(), low, high);
    else if (root->value() < low)
      PRINT_RANGE(root->rightchild(), low, high);
    else {
      PRINT_RANGE(root->leftchild(), low, high);
      PRINT(root->value());
      PRINT_RANGE(root->rightchild(), low, high);
    }
}
```

5.20 The corresponding array will be in the following order (equivalent to level order for the heap):

$$12 \quad 9 \quad 10 \quad 5 \quad 4 \quad 1 \quad 8 \quad 7 \quad 3 \quad 2$$

5.21 **(a)** The array will take on the following order:

$$6 \quad 5 \quad 3 \quad 4 \quad 2 \quad 1$$

The value 7 will be at the end of the array.

(b) The array will take on the following order:

$$7 \quad 4 \quad 6 \quad 3 \quad 2 \quad 1$$

The value 5 will be at the end of the array.

```
5.22  heap::heap(ELEM* h, int num, int max)    // Constructor
        { Heap = h;  n = num;  size = max;  buildheap(); }

      int heap::heapsize() const // Return current size of heap
        { return n; }

      bool heap::isLeaf(int pos) const
        { return (pos >= n/2) && (pos < n); }

      // Return position for left child of pos
      int heap::leftchild(int pos) const {
        assert(pos < n/2);  // Must be a pos with a left child
        return 2*pos + 1;
      }

      // Return position for right child of pos
      int heap::rightchild(int pos) const {
        assert(pos < (n-1)/2); // Must be pos with a left child
        return 2*pos + 2;
      }

      int heap::parent(int pos) const { // Return pos for parent
        assert(pos > 0); return (pos-1)/2; // Pos must have parent
      }

      void heap::insert(const ELEM val) { // Insert val in heap
        assert(n < size);
        int curr = n++;
        Heap[curr] = val;                  // Start at end of heap
        // Now sift up until curr's parent > curr
        while ((curr!=0) &&
               (key(Heap[curr]) > key(Heap[parent(curr)]))) {
          swap(Heap[curr], Heap[parent(curr)]);
          curr = parent(curr);
      }}

      ELEM heap::removemax() {            // Remove maximum value
        assert(n > 0);
        swap(Heap[0], Heap[--n]); // Swap maximum with last value
        if (n != 0)     // Not on last element
          siftdown(0);  // Put new heap root val in correct place
        return Heap[n];
      }
```

6

General Trees

6.1 ```
\\ Return TRUE iff t1 and t2 are roots of identical trees
bool Compare(GTNode* t1, GTNode* t2) {
  GTNode *c1, *c2;
  if (((t1 == NULL) && (t2 != NULL)) ||
      ((t2 == NULL) && (t1 != NULL)))
    return FALSE;
  if ((t1 == NULL) && (t2 == NULL)) return TRUE;
  if (t1->value() != t2->value()) return FALSE;
  c1 = t1->leftmost_child();
  c2 = t2->leftmost_child();
  while(!((c1 == NULL) && (c2 == NULL))) {
    if (!Compare(c1, c2)) return FALSE;
    if (c1 != NULL) c1 = c1->right_sibling();
    if (c2 != NULL) c2 = c2->right_sibling();
}}
```

6.2 ```
\\ Return TRUE iff t1 and t2 are roots of identical trees
bool Compare2(BinNode* t1, BinNode* t2) {
  BinNode *c1, *c2;
  if (((t1 == NULL) && (t2 != NULL)) ||
      ((t2 == NULL) && (t1 != NULL)))
    return FALSE;
  if ((t1 == NULL) && (t2 == NULL)) return TRUE;
  if (t1->value() != t2->value()) return FALSE;
  if (Compare2(t1->leftchild(), t2->leftchild()))
    if (Compare2(t1->rightchild(), t2->rightchild()))
      return TRUE;
  if (Compare2(t1->leftchild(), t2->rightchild()))
    if (Compare2(t1->rightchild(), t2->leftchild))
      return TRUE;
  return FALSE;
}
```

6.3
```
void postprint(GTNode* rt) {
    if (rt == NULL) return;
    GTNode* temp = rt->leftmost_child();
    while (temp != NULL)
        { postprint(temp);  temp = temp->right_sibling(); }
    if (rt->isLeaf()) cout << "Leaf: ";
    else cout << "Internal: ";
    cout << rt->value() << "\n";  // Print or take other action
}
```

6.4
```
int gencount(GTNode* rt) { // Preorder traversal from the root
    int count = 1;
    if (rt == NULL) return 0
    GTNode* temp = rt->leftmost_child();
    while (temp != NULL) {
        count += gencount(temp);
        temp = temp->right_sibling();
    }
    return count;
}
```

6.5 The Weighted Union Rule says that when two parent-pointer trees are merged, the smaller one's root becomes a child of the larger one's root. Thus, we need to keep track of the number of nodes in a tree. To do so, modify the node array to store an integer value with each node. Initially, each node is in its own tree, so the weights for each node begin as 1. Whenever we wish to merge two trees, check the weights of the roots to determine which has more nodes. Then, add to the weight of the final root the weight of the new subtree.

6.6

0	1	2	3	4	5	6	7	8	9	10	11	12	13	14	15
-1	0	0	0	0	0	0	6	0	0	0	9	0	0	12	0

6.7 For eight nodes labeled 0 through 7, use the following series of equivalences:

(0, 1) (2, 3) (4, 5) (6, 7) (4 6) (0, 2) (4 0)

This requires checking fourteen parent pointers (two for each equivalence), but none are actually followed since these are all roots. It is possible to double the number of parent pointers checked by choosing direct children of roots in each case.

6.8 For the "lists of Children" representation, every node stores a data value and a pointer to its list of children. Further, every child (every node except the root) has a record associated with it containing an index and a pointer. Indicating the size of the data value as D, the size of a pointer as P and the size of an index as I, the overhead fraction is

$$\frac{3P + I}{D + 3P + I}.$$

For the "Left Child/Right Sibling" representation, every node stores three pointers and a data value, for an overhead fraction of

$$\frac{3P}{D + 3P}.$$

The first linked representation of Section 6.3.3 stores with each node a data value and a size field (denoted by S). Each child (every node except the root) also has a pointer pointing to it. The overhead fraction is thus

$$\frac{S + P}{D + S + P}$$

making it quite efficient.

The second linked representation of Section 6.3.3 stores with each node a data value and a pointer to the list of children. Each child (every node except the root) has two additional pointers associated with it to indicate its place on the parent's linked list. Thus, the overhead fraction is

$$\frac{3P}{D + 3P}.$$

6.9
```
BinNode* convert(GTNode* genroot) {
    if (genroot == NULL) return NULL;
    GTNode* gtemp = genroot->leftmost_child();
    btemp = new BinNode(genroot->value(), convert(gtemp),
                   convert(genroot->right_sibling())));
}
```

6.10
- Parent$(r) = (r - 1)/k$ if $0 < r < n$.
- Ith child$(r) = kr + I$ if $kr + I < n$.
- Left sibling$(r) = r - 1$ if $r \bmod k \neq 1$ $0 < r < n$.
- Right sibling$(r) = r + 1$ if $r \bmod k \neq 0$ and $r + 1 < n$.

6.11 **(a)** The overhead fraction is

$$\frac{4(k + 1)}{4 + 4(k + 1)}.$$

(b) The overhead fraction is

$$\frac{4k}{16 + 4k}.$$

(c) The overhead fraction is

$$\frac{4(k+2)}{16 + 4(k+2)}.$$

(d) The overhead fraction is

$$\frac{2k}{2k + 4}.$$

6.12 Base Case: The number of leaves in a non-empty tree of 0 internal nodes is $(K - 1)0 + 1 = 1$. Thus, the theorem is correct in the base case.

Induction Hypothesis: Assume that the theorem is correct for any full K-ary tree containing n internal nodes.

Induction Step: Add K children to an arbitrary leaf node of the tree with n internal nodes. This new tree now has 1 more internal node, and $K - 1$ more leaf nodes, so theorem still holds. Thus, the theorem is correct, by the principle of Mathematical Induction.

6.13 **(a)** $CA/BG///FEDD///H/I//$

(b) $C'A'/B'G/F'E'D/H'/I$

6.14
```
    X
    |
    P
  -----
  | | |
  C Q R
    ---
    | |
    V M
```

6.15 **(a)**
```
    // Use a helper function with a pass-by-reference variable
    // to indicate current position in the node list.
    BinNode* convert(char* inlist) {
      int curr = 0;
      return converthelp(inlist, curr);
    }

    // As converthelp processes the node list, curr is
    // incremented appropriately.
    BinNode* converthelp(char* inlist, int& curr) {
      if (inlist[curr] == '/') {
        curr++;
        return NULL;
      }
      BinNode temp = new BinNode(inlist[curr++], NULL, NULL);
      temp->left = converthelp(inlist, curr);
      temp->right = converthelp(inlist, curr);
      return temp;
    }
```

(b)
```
    // Use a helper function with a pass-by-reference variable
    // to indicate current position in the node list.
    BinNode* convert(char* inlist) {
      int curr = 0;
      return converthelp(inlist, curr);
    }

    // As converthelp processes the node list, curr is
    // incremented appropriately.
    BinNode* converthelp(char* inlist, int& curr) {
      if (inlist[curr] == '/') {
        curr++;
        return NULL;
      }
      BinNode temp = new BinNode(inlist[curr++], NULL, NULL);
      if (inlist[curr] == '\'') return temp;
      curr++ // Eat the internal node mark.
      temp->left = converthelp(inlist, curr);
      temp->right = converthelp(inlist, curr);
      return temp;
    }
```

```
(c)  // Use a helper function with a pass-by-reference variable
     // to indicate current position in the node list.
     GTNode* convert(char* inlist) {
       int curr = 0;
       return converthelp(inlist, curr);
     }

     // As converthelp processes the node list, curr is
     // incremented appropriately.
     GTNode* converthelp(char* inlist, int& curr) {
       if (inlist[curr] == ')') {
         curr++;
         return NULL;
       }
       GTNode temp = new GTNode(inlist[curr++]);
       if (curr == ')') {
         temp->insert_first(NULL);
         return temp;
       }
       temp->insert_first(converthelp(inlist, curr));
       while (curr != ')')
         temp->insert_next(converthelp(inlist, curr));
       curr++;
       return temp;
     }
```

6.16 The Huffman tree is a full binary tree. To decode, we do not need to know the weights of nodes, only the letter values stored in the leaf nodes. Thus, we can use a coding much like that of Equation 6.2, storing only a bit mark for internal nodes, and a bit mark and letter value for leaf nodes.

7

Graphs

7.1 Base Case: A graph with 1 vertex has $1(1-1)/2 = 0$ edges. Thus, the theorem holds in the base case.

Induction Hypothesis: A graph with n vertices has at most $n(n-1)/2$ edges.

Induction Step: Add a new vertex to a graph of n vertices. The most edges that can be added is n, by connecting the new vertex to each of the old vertices, with the maximum number of edges occurring in the complete graph. Thus,

$$E(n+1) \geq E(n) + n \geq n(n-1)/2 + n = (n^2 + n)/2 = n(n+1)/2.$$

By the principle of Mathematical Induction, the theorem is correct.

7.2 **(a)** For a graph of n vertices to be connected, clearly at least $|\mathbf{V}| - \mathbf{1}$ edges are required since each edge serves to add one more vertex to the connected component. No cycles means that no additional edges are given, yielding exactly $|\mathbf{V}| - \mathbf{1}$ edges.

(b) Proof by contradiction. If the graph is not connected, then by definition there are at least two components. At least one of these components has i vertices with i or more edges (by the pigeonhole principle). Given $i-1$ edges to connect the component, the ith edge must then directly connect two of the vertices already connected through the other edges. The result is a cycle. Thus, to avoid a cycle, the graph must be connected.

7.3 (a)

```
        1    2    3    4    5    6
      --------------------------
  1 |      10        20        2  |
  2 | 10        3    5            |
  3 |      3             15       |
  4 | 20   5             11   10  |
  5 |           15   11        3  |
  6 | 2              10   3       |
      --------------------------
```

(b)

```
1 -> 2(10)  -> 4(20)  -> 6(2)   -> \
2 -> 1(10)  -> 3(3)   -> 4(5)   -> \
3 -> 2(3)   -> 5(15)  -> \
4 -> 1(20)  -> 2(5)   -> 5(11)  -> 6(10) -> \
5 -> 3(15)  -> 4(11)  -> 6(3)   -> \
6 -> 1(2)   -> 4(10)  -> 5(3)   -> \
```

(c) The adjacency matrix requires $36 \times 2 = 72$ bytes. The adjacency list requires $24 \times 4 + 18 \times (2 + 2) = 168$ bytes. Thus, the matrix is considerably more efficient in this case.

7.4
```
1 -> 2   6   4
     |   ^   ^
     V    \  |
     3 --> 5
```

7.5
```
1 -> 2 -> 3
|\
V \
6  V
   4 -> 5
```

7.6 Add the following at the end of algorithm on Page 206:

```
// Check for cycles
for (v=0; v<G.n(); v++)
  if (Count[v] != 0)
    cout << "This vertex is part of a cycle: " << v << "\n";
```

7.7

	1	2	3	4	5	6
Initial	∞	∞	∞	0	∞	∞
Process 4	20	5	∞	0	11	10
Process 2	15	5	8	0	11	10
Process 3	15	5	8	0	11	10
Process 6	12	5	8	0	11	10
Process 5	12	5	8	0	11	10
Process 1	12	5	8	0	11	10

7.8 Store at each position of the array both the distance, and the neighbor through which the vertex is reached (the vertex's parent in the DFS tree). At the end, print out the path, in reverse order back to the source.

```
// Compute shortest path distances
void Dijkstra(Graph& G, int s) {
  Rec D[G.n()];
  for (int i=0; i<G.n(); i++)        // Initialize
    D[i].dist = INFINITY;
  D[s].dist = 0; D[s].par = -1; // This is the root
  for (i=0; i<G.n(); i++) {          // Process the vertices
    int v = minVertex(G, D);
    G.Mark[v] = VISITED;
    if (D[v].dist == INFINITY)
      return; // Remaining vertices unreachable
    for (Edge w = G.first(v); G.isEdge(w); w = G.next(w))
      if (D[G.v2(w)].dist > (D[v].dist + G.weight(w))) {
        D[G.v2(w)].dist = D[v].dist + G.weight(w);
        D[G.v2(w)].par = v; // w's parent in the DFS is v
      }
  }
  // Print out the paths (in reverse order)
  for (i=0; i<G.n(); i++) {
    cout << "Path for " << i << ": ";
    for (t=i; D[t].par != -1; t = D[t].par)
      cout << t << " ";
    cout << s << "\n";
  }
}
```

```
int minVertex(Graph& G, Rec* D) { // Find min cost vertex
  int v;  // Initialize v to any unvisited vertex;
  for (int i=0; i<G.n(); i++)
    if (G.Mark[i] == UNVISITED) { v = i; break; }
  for (i=0; i<G.n(); i++)  // Now find smallest value
    if ((G.Mark[i] == UNVISITED) && (D[i].dist < D[v].dist))
      v = i;
  return v;
}
```

7.9 Here is a pseudo-code sketch of the algorithm. Converting to C++ is quite easy since the code is given in the book as described here.

```
INITIALIZE array Count to 0's;
FOR every edge (v, w) // Similar to BFS topological sort
  Count[w]++;
IF the number of vertices with zero Count is not 1
  THEN return "No Root";
ELSE {
  do DFS search from the vertex with zero Count;
  Verify that every vertex has been marked;
}
```

7.10 The following algorithm is $O(|\mathbf{V}| + |\mathbf{E}|)$. It is a minor modification on DFS.

```
// V is the root of the DAG.
int DAGdepth(Graph& G, int v, int depth) {// Depth first search
  int currmax = depth;
  for (Edge w = G.first(v); G.isEdge(w); w = G.next(w)) {
    if (G.Mark[G.v2(w)] == VISITED) ERROR; // Not a DAG.
    currmax = MAX(DAGdepth(G, G.v2(w), depth+1), currmax);
  }
  return currmax;
}
```

7.11 To solve this problem, simply run the BFS topological sort algorithm. If there are any cycles, then some vertices will remain in the queue.

7.12 To solve this problem, simply run the standard DFS algorithm, returning the fact that there is a cycle if any already visited vertex is encountered. This algorithm has has time $O(n)$ because the graph can only have $O(n-1)$ edges if it does not contain a cycle, and any existing cycle will be detected in at most n edge visits.

7.13 Simply reverse the direction of all the edges, then run the standard algorithm for Single-Source Shortest Paths.

7.14 O-paths:

```
    2   3   4   5   6
1  10   x  20   x   2
2       3   5   x   x
3           x  15   x
4              11  10
5                   3
```

1-paths:

```
    2   3   4   5   6
1  10   x  20   x   2
2       3   5   x  12
3           x  15   x
4              11  10
5                   3
```

2-paths:

```
    2   3   4   5   6
1  10  13  15   x   2
2       3   5   x  12
3           8  15  15
4              11  10
5                   3
```

3-paths:

```
    2   3   4   5   6
1  10  13  15   x   2
2       3   5  18  12
3           8  15   x
4              11  10
5                   3
```

4-paths:

	2	3	4	5	6
1	10	13	15	31	2
2		3	5	16	12
3			8	15	15
4				11	10
5					3

5-paths:

	2	3	4	5	6
1	10	13	15	31	2
2		3	5	16	12
3			8	15	15
4				11	10
5					3

6-paths:

	2	3	4	5	6
1	10	13	12	6	2
2		3	5	16	12
3			8	15	15
4				11	10
5					3

7.15 The problem is that each entry of the array is set independently, forcing processing of the adjacency list repeatedly from the beginning. This illustrates the dangers involved in thoughtlessly using an inefficient access member to a data structure implementation. A better solution is to process the actual edges within the graph. In other words, for each vertex, visit its adjacency list. Set the shortest-paths array by setting the values associated with that edge. If the array is initialized with values of ∞, then any vertices not connected by an edge will retain that value.

7.16 Clearly the algorithm requires at least $\Omega(n^2)$ time since this much information must be produced in the end. A stronger lower bound is difficult to obtain, and certainly beyond the ability of students at this level. The primary goal of this exercise is for the students to demonstrate understanding of the concept of a lower bound on a problem, in a context where they will not be able to make the lower bound and the algorithm's upper bound meet.

7.17 (3, 2) (2, 4) (2, 1) (1, 6) (6, 5).

Alternatively, (3, 2) (2, 4) (4, 6) (6, 1) (6, 5).

7.18

```
            1  2  3  4  5  6
Initial   -1 -1 -1 -1 -1 -1
(1, 6)    -1 -1 -1 -1 -1  1
(2, 3)    -1 -1  2 -1 -1  1   (Alt: (6, 5))
(6, 5)    -1 -1  2 -1  1  1
(1, 2)    -1  1  2 -1  1  1   (Alt: (6, 4))
(6, 4)    -1  1  2  1  1  1
```

7.19 Simply use any Minimal Cost Spanning Tree algorithm, but alway pick the greatest edge among the available choices instead of the least edge.

7.20 The two algorithms can yield different spanning trees only if they make different choices regarding equal-valued edges. For example, the answers to Exercises 7.17 and 7.18 indicate that choices can be made, leading to different spanning trees with the same total value.

7.21 The proof that Prim's algorithm is correct serves as a proof for this theorem, since, when the edge values are distinct, Prim's algorithm has only one series of alternatives, leading to one unique tree.

7.22 If all of the edges are negative, then a smaller number is obtained by picking more edges than necessary to span the graph. It is not clear what the desired answer should be – (1) the smallest value that spans the graph, even if it is not a tree, or (2)the smallest value with the minimum number of edges required to span the tree. If (1), then neither algorithm works since both will give spanning trees, not the graph that spans but with least value. If (2), then the algorithms work.

7.23 Dijkstra's algorithm does yield a spanning tree. However, this spanning tree is not necessarily of least cost. Consider the example:

```
      A
  4 / \ 3
   /   \
  B-----C
     2
```

The MST is (A, C) (B, C) for cost 5. But, if starting at A, Dijkstra's algorithm will pick (A, C) (A, B) since by that way B is closer.

7.24 Use a variation on Kruskal's algorithm. Process the edges in any order, merging two equivalence classes if they contain vertices joined by an edge. At the end, each equivalence class is a connected component.

8

Internal Sorting

8.1 Base Case: For the list of one element, the double loop is not executed and the list is not processed. Thus, the list of one element remains unaltered and is sorted.

Induction Hypothesis: Assume that the list of n elements is sorted correctly by Insertion Sort.

Induction Step: The list of $n + 1$ elements is processed by first sorting the top n elements. By the induction hypothesis, this is done correctly. The final pass of the outer `for` loop will process the last element (call it X). This is done by the inner `for` loop, which moves X up the list until a value smaller than that of X is encountered. At this point, X has been properly inserted into the sorted list, leaving the entire collection of $n + 1$ elements correctly sorted. Thus, by the principle of Mathematical Induction, the theorem is correct.

8.2
```
void StackSort(Stack& IN) {
  Stack Temp1, Temp2;

  while (!IN.isEmpty()) // Transfer everything to another stack
    Temp1.push(IN.pop());
  IN.push(Temp1.pop());  // Put back one element
  while (!Temp1.isEmpty()) { // Process rest of the elements
    while (IN.top() > Temp1.top()) // Find the element's place
      Temp2.push(IN.pop());
    IN.push(Temp1.pop());    // Put the element in
    while (!Temp2.isEmpty()) // Put the rest back
      IN.push(Temp2.pop());
  }
}
```

8.3 The revised algorithm will work correctly, and its asymptotic complexity will remain $\Theta(n^2)$. However, it will do about twice as many comparisons, since it will compare adjacent elements within the portion of the list already known to be sorted. These additional comparisons are unproductive.

8.4 While binary search will find the proper place to locate the next element, it will still be necessary to move the intervening elements down one position in the array. This requires the same number of operations as a sequential search. However, it does reduce the number of element/element comparisons, and may be somewhat faster by a constant factor since shifting several elements may be more efficient than an equal number of swap operations.

8.5 **(a)**
```
void selsort(ELEM* array, int n) { // Selection Sort
    for (int i=0; i<n-1; i++) {       // Select i'th record
      int lowindex = i;               // Remember its index
      for (int j=n-1; j>i; j--)       // Find the least value
        if (key(array[j]) < key(array[lowindex]))
          lowindex = j;               // Put it in place
      if (i != lowindex)  // Add this check for the exercise
        swap(array[i], array[lowindex]);
    }
}
```

(b) There is unlikely to be much improvement; more likely the algorithm will slow down. This is because the time spent checking (n times) is unlikely to save enough swaps to make up.

(c) Try it and see!

8.6
- Insertion Sort is stable. A swap is done only if the lower element's value is LESS.

- Bubble Sort is stable. A swap is done only if the lower element's value is LESS.

- Selection Sort is NOT stable. The new low value is set only if it is actually less than the previous one, but the direction of the search is from the bottom of the array. The algorithm will be stable if "less than" in the check becomes "less than or equal to" for selecting the low key position.

- Selection Sort is NOT stable. The sublist sorts are done independently, and it is quite possible to swap an element in one sublist ahead of its equal value in another sublist. Once they are in the same sublist, they will retain this (incorrect) relationship.

- Quick-sort is NOT stable. After selecting the pivot, it is swapped with the last element. This action can easily put equal records out of place.

- Conceptually (in particular, the linked list version) Mergesort is stable. The array implementations are NOT stable, since, given that the sublists are stable, the merge operation will pick the element from the lower list before the upper list if they are equal. This is easily modified to replace "less than" with "less than or equal to."

- Heapsort is NOT stable. Elements in separate sides of the heap are processed independently, and could easily become out of relative order.

- Binsort is stable. Equal values that come later are appended to the list.

- Radix Sort is stable. While the processing is from bottom to top, the bins are also filled from bottom to top, preserving relative order.

8.7 In the worst case, the stack can store n records. This can be cut to $\log n$ in the worst case by putting the larger partition on FIRST, followed by the smaller. Thus, the smaller will be processed first, cutting the size of the next stacked partition by at least half.

8.8 **(a)** Each call to qsort costs $\Theta(i \log i)$. Thus, the total cost is

$$\sum_{i=1}^{n} i \log i = \Theta(n^2 \log n).$$

(b) Each call to qsort costs $\Theta(n \log n)$ for length(L) $= n$, so the total cost is $\Theta(n^2 \log n)$.

8.9
```
typedef ELEM char*;
// Only the partition function need be changed.
int partition(ELEM* array, int l, int r, KEY pivot) {
  do {                    // Move the bounds inward until they meet
    while (strcmp(array[++l], pivot) < 0); // Move bound right
    // Move right bound left
    while (r && (strcmp(array[--r], pivot) < 0));
    swap(array[l], array[r]);      // Swap out-of-place values
  } while (l < r);                 // Stop when they cross
  swap(array[l], array[r]);        // Reverse last, wasted swap
  return l;        // Return first position in right partition
}
```

8.10 For $n = 1000$, $n^2 = 1,000,000$, $n^{1.5} = 1000 * \sqrt{1000} \approx 32,000$, and $n \log n \approx 10,000$. So, the constant factor for Shellsort can be anything less than about 32 times that of Insertion Sort for Shellsort to be faster. The constant factor for Shellsort can be anything less than about 100 times that of Insertion Sort for Quicksort to be faster.

8.11 **(a)** The worst case occurs when all of the sublists are of size 1, except for one list of size $i - k + 1$. If this happens on each call to SPLITk, then the total cost of the algorithm will be $\Theta(n^2)$.

(b) In the average case, the lists are split into k sublists of roughly equal length. Thus, the total cost is $\Theta(n \log_k n)$.

8.12 (This question comes from Rawlins.) Clearly we can't do better than $\Theta(n \log n)$ comparisons, because we would otherwise be able to devise a general-purpose sorting algorithm that is faster than $\Theta(n \log n)$. The question is whether we can devise an algorithm to do sorting as fast as $\Theta(n \log n)$. Here is an algorithm similar to Quicksort. Pick a nut. It can be used to partition the bolts into a group smaller than the nut and a group larger. If there is a bolt for every nut, then there is a bolt that fits exactly. This bolt in turn can partition the nuts. We now have equal sized groups of small nut and bolts, and large nuts and bolts. These can be sorted recursively.

A more complicated algorithm similar to Mergesort can be devised. Pair up nuts and bolts at random. Compare each pair. Then merge adjacent pairs, to "sort" into groups. Of course, you may have two nuts or two bolts that can't be directly compared, but the nuts can be compared to the bolts and vice versa. Keep merging the runs together until complete.

Thus, $\Theta(n \log n)$ comparison algorithms are possible, so the problem has cost $\Theta(n \log n)$ comparisons.

8.13 Consider Mergesort in terms of a full binary tree. Each call to Mergesort either results in two new calls to Mergesort, or else a single call to Insertion Sort. Thus, the calls to Insertion Sort are equivalent to the leaf nodes of a full binary tree. We know from the Full Binary Tree Theorem that the number of leaf nodes in a full binary tree of n nodes is $\lceil n/2 \rceil$. Thus, if there are n calls to Mergesort, there will be $\lceil n/2 \rceil$ calls to Insertion Sort.

8.14 For this problem, a Binsort is ideal. In fact, we can keep the memory down to only 30,000 bits by storing a single bit for each value in the range. Read the numbers in sequential order and mark the ith bit for a number i. At the end, merely write out the numbers, in order, whose bits are marked.

8.15 (a) This can be done directly in $\Theta(n)$ worst case time without sorting.

   (b) This can be done directly in $\Theta(n)$ worst case time without sorting.

   (c) This can be done directly in $\Theta(n)$ worst case time without sorting.

   (d) Sorting allows this to be done in $\Theta(n \log n)$ time by first sorting and then selecting the value in the middle position. However, it is possible to use a variation on Quicksort to do this in $\Theta(n)$ time in the average case. (Most students at this level will not be familiar with that median selection algorithm, however).

   (e) This is best done by sorting, then making a pass through the array keeping track of the item seen the most times.

8.16 (a) For 3 values, use the following series of if statements (based on the decision tree concept of Figure 8.16, and optimized for swaps).

```
void Sort3(ELEM A) { // Assume A has 3 elements
  if (A[1] < A[0])
    if (A[2] < A[0])
      if (A[2] < A[1])    // ZYX
        swap(A[0], A[2]);
      else {              // YZX
        swap(A[0], A[1]);
        swap(A[1], A[2]);
      }
    else                  // YXZ
      swap(A[0], A[1]);
  else
    if (A[2] < A[1])
      if (A[2] < A[1]) { // ZXY
        swap(A[0], A[2]);
        swap(A[1], A[2]);
      }
      else                // XZY
        swap(A[1], A[2]);
    else                  // XYZ -- Do nothing
}
```

Cost:

Best case: 2 compares.

Avg case: $16/6 = 2\ 2/3$ compares.

Worst case: 3 compares.

(b) Doing a similar approach of building a decision tree for 5 numbers is somewhat overwhelming since there are 120 permutations. A pretty good algorithm can be had be building on Sort3 from part (a). Use Sort3 to sort the first 3 numbers. Then, add the 4th number in 2 comparisons by checking the middle of the first 3, and then checking the 1st or 3rd as appropriate. The last number can be added using at most 3 comparisons by checking the 2nd of the first 4 numbers, then (at worst) the 3rd and 4th. Thus, the total number of comparisons is at most 8. The best case is 6, the average case is 7 4/15 (2 2/3 for the first 3 numbers, exactly 2 for the 4th number and 2 3/5 for the 5th number).

It is possible to do this in 7 comparisons, worst case. Seek Knuth, Volume 3.

(c) Call the algorithm from part (b) Sort5. Use it to sort the first 5 numbers in at most 8 comparisons. Now, add in the sixth number by first checking the 3rd position, and then 2 more comparisons as necessary. Likewise, number 7 can be added with at most 3 comparisons and number 8 needs at most 3 comparisons. So, the worst case is 17. The best case is 13.

There is an algorithm that can do this in 16 comparisons for the worst case. See Knuth, Volume 3.

8.17
```
list mergesort(list inlist) {
  list templist[2];
  if (inlist.length() <= 1) return inlist;
  inlist.setFirst();
  int curr = 0;
  // Split the elements among two sublists lists
  while (!inlist.isEmpty()) {
    ELEM item = inlist.remove();
    templist[curr].append(item);
    curr = (curr + 1) % 2;
  }
  mergesort(templist[0]);
  mergesort(templist[1]);
  // Now, merge the lists together
  templist[0].setFirst();
  templist[1].setFirst();
  while (!templist[0].isEmpty() || !templist[1].isEmpty()) {
    if (templist[0].isEmpty()) {
      item = templist[1].remove();
      inlist.append(item);
```

```
    }
    else if (templist[1].isEmpty()) {
      item = templist[0].remove();
      inlist.append(item);
    }
    else if (templist[0].currValue() <
            templist[1].currValue()) {
      item = templist[0].remove();
      inlist.append(item);
    }
    else {
      item = templist[1].remove();
      inlist.append(item);
    }
  }
  return inlist;
}
```

8.18 There are n possible choices for the position of a given element in the array. Any search algorithm based on comparisons can be modeled using a decision tree. The tree must have at least n leaf nodes, one for each of the possible choices for solution. A tree with n leaves must have depth at least $\log n$. Thus, any search algorithm based on comparisons requires at least $\log n$ work in the worst case.

9

File Processing and External Sorting

9.1 Clearly the prices continue to change. RAM in particular has had a price drop in time between when I wrote the text and when I am writing these solutions at the end of 1996. But, the principles remain the same.

9.2 The first question is How many tracks are required by the file? A track holds $64 * .5K = 32K$. Thus, the file requires 4 tracks. The time to read a track is seek time to the track + latency time + (interleaf factor × rotation time). Seek time to the first track is is on average 1/3 the time to cross the disk, or 20 ms $+0.3$ ms $* 128/3 \approx 32.8$ ms. Latency time is $0.5*16.7$ ms, and track rotation time is 16.7 ms for a total time to read the first track of

$$32.8 + 4.5 * 16.7 \approx 107.8 \text{ ms.}$$

Seek time for the remaining three tracks is 20.3 ms, with identical latency and read times. Thus, the total file read time is

$$107.8 + 3(20.3 + 4.5 * 16.7) \approx 393.7$$

which is pretty slow by today's standards.

9.3 Considering all of the possible cases for a disk with n tracks, the first track could be at any position from 1 to n, and the second track could be at any position from 1 to n. If the first track is i and the second is j, then the distance is $|j - i|$. Alternatively, in n of the n^2 possible cases the distance is 0, and otherwise we can count only the cases where

$i < j$ and multiply the sum by two to account for the cases where $j < i$. Thus, we get the average cost as

$$2\frac{\sum_{i=1}^{n}\sum_{j=i+1}^{n}(j-i)}{n^2} \quad =$$

$$2\frac{\sum_{i=1}^{n-1}\sum_{j=1}^{i}(j)}{n^2} \quad =$$

$$2\frac{\sum_{i=1}^{n-1}(i^2+i)/2}{n^2} \quad =$$

$$\frac{1}{n^2}(\sum_{i=1}^{n-1} i^2 + i) \quad =$$

$$\frac{1}{n^2}(\frac{2n^3+3n^2+n}{6} + \frac{3n^2+3n}{6}) \quad =$$

$$\frac{2n^3+6n^2+4n}{6n^2} \quad \approx \quad n/3.$$

9.4 This is quite similar to Exercise 9.2, but with more modern equipment. One track holds 31.5K bytes, so the file requires 4 tracks plus 4 sectors of a fifth track. Seek time to the first track is 3 ms $+2100/3*0.08$ ms $\approx$ $59ms$. Latency and read time together require $3.5*8.33$ ms. Thus, the time to read the first track is about 88 ms. The time to read the next three tracks is $3+2100/3*0.08+3.5*8.33 \approx 32.2$ ms. The last track takes just as long to read since it requires three rotations to read the 4 blocks. Thus, the total time required is $88+32.2*4 = 216.8$ ms.

9.5 A record of 160 bytes requires 160 bytes/6250 bpi $= 0.0256$ inches of tape. Since the interblock gap is 0.3 inches, a block and a gap must sum to 3 inches, leaving 2.7 inches of data, or at least 106 records/block.

9.6 (a) Assuming that the 20 ms time to search a block is primarily limited by the CPU speed, and given a probability of hitting the cache around half of the time, doubling the CPU can speed up the application by at most 20/70 % (derived from an average record fetch requiring 50 ms of I/O and 20 ms of CPU time). In fact, it is almost certain that the bulk of the 20 ms is spent in memory access, and speeding the CPU will have marginal effect.

(b) From the analysis of the previous section, I/O time takes about 50/70 of the work. Cutting the I/O time in half will cut the expected access time to about 45 ms, a savings of slightly over 35% of the time.

    (c) Doubling the bufferpool size will mean that most requests will hit the bufferpool, maybe as much as 90% of the time. This cuts the expected time to about 30 ms, a savings of about 55-60%.

9.7 The batch method is more efficient when enough sectors are visited to make processing the whole file in sequential order more efficient. Since the file consists of 10,000 sectors, it requires 50,000 ms to process sequentially. This is equivalent to random access to 1000 sectors. Thus, if the set of queries requires processing more than 1000 sectors, it would be more efficient to process the entire file in batch mode.

9.8 **(a)** 10 4 6 8 5

    (b) 5 (6 times) 3 (3 times) 4 (1 time) 6 (1 time) 8 (1 time)

    (c) 5 (6 times) 3 (3 times) 9 (3 times) 2 (3 times) 8 (2 times)

    (d) 5 8 6 4 10

9.9 Since working memory is 1MB and the block size is 1KB, the number of blocks in working memory is 1024. The expected runlength is 2MB, and 1024 runs can be merged in a single multiway merge operation. Thus, the largest expected file size for a single pass of multiway merge is 2 Gigabytes.

9.10 Since working memory is 256KB and the blocksize is 8KB, the working memory holds 32 blocks. The expected runlength is 512KB, so a single pass of multiway merge forms runs of length 16MB. The second pass then forms a run as large as 512MB.

9.11 This proposition is TRUE. If a record X is preceded by less than M keys larger than it, then X will gain entry into the heap prior to any of the keys larger than it being output. Thus, X will be output. Since this condition holds for all records, all records are output in sorted order.

9.12 As illustrated by Exercise 9.9, reasonable use of memory should allow this file to be sorted after a single execution of replacement selection followed by a single execution of multi-way merge. In practice, this means reading and writing every record twice, with random block access. If average block access time is estimated to be 10 ms, and the file consists of 4K blocks, the file has around 25,000 blocks. Thus, the entire operation takes about $4 * 25000 * .01 = 1000$ sec which is a bit over 15 minutes. This is not unreasonable in comparison with the third line of Table 9.12, considering that disks are now faster than that used for the table.

9.13 **(a)** Speeding up the CPU will have little effect on an external sorting operation.

(b) Cutting the disk I/O time will substantially improve the external sorting time. A reasonable estimate is that cutting disk I/O time in half will cut the sorting time by around 1/3.

(c) Main memory access time will not help a great deal, since disk I/O is the probable bottleneck. However, for the sorting operation, main memory access time is in fact more of a bottleneck than CPU speed, so it should help more to speed the memory than to speed the CPU.

(d) Increasing the memory size by a factor of two will increase the file size that can be processed by a single pass of multi-way merge by a factor of four, in two passes by a factor of eight, and so no. If this leads to a reduction in the number of passes need to process the file, then a substantial time savings will be realized. This could easily cut the processing time by 1/3 or 1/4 since 2 or 3 passes of multiway merge under the initial conditions are reasonable to expect.

9.14 How to approach this depends on the form of the records. If they have relatively small, fixed-length keys, the best solution would be to make a simple linear index file, as discussed in Chapter 11. Simply make a pass through the original record file and store in the index file for each record the key and a pointer to the original record. Then, sort the index file.

If the records to be sorted have a large, variable length key, the index file approach will not work. In this case, it is possible to sort the file directly. We must modify both replacement selection and multi-way merge. For replacement selection, we should still use the concept of an index in the heap. The heap stores fixed length pointers to a pool of variable length records read into memory. To compare two elements in the heap, go back to the records in the pool. In this way the heap can be manipulated without disturbing the pool. As records are processed, read them out of the pool. Compacting the pool or some similar memory management concept (Chapter 12) will be necessary. For multiway merge, simply read in as many records as will fit into each run's memory space, and refill as necessary. The merge process itself remains unchanged, except that a suitable compare function will be required.

10

Searching

10.1
```
int dictsrch(int K, int* array, int left, int right,
             int low, int high) {
  // left and right are array bounds.  low and high are
  // key range bounds.  Return position of the element in
  // array (if any) with value K
  int i;
  double fract;
  int l = left-1;
  int r = right+1;     // l and r are beyond bounds of the array
  if (K == high)       // Special case
    if (K == array[right}) return right;
    else return UNSUCCESSFUL;
  while (r != l+1) {    // Stop when l and r meet
    // Compute where in the current range K will be
    fract = (double)(K - low)/(double)(high - low);
    // Set position to check at that fraction of array bounds
    i = l+1 + (int)(fract * (double)(r - l - 1));
    // i will be between l and r, non-inclusive,
    // so progress must be made
    // Now, check that position and update ranges
    if (K < array[i])
      { r = i; high = array[i]; }
    if (K == array[i]) return i;
    if (K > array[i])
      { l = i; low = array[i]; }
  }
  return UNSUCCESSFUL; // key value not found
}
```

10.2 The partition and findpivot functions remain the same.

```
void findK(ELEM* array, int i, int j, ELEM K) {
  int pivotindex = findpivot(array, i, j);
  swap(array[pivotindex], array[j]);    // Stick pivot at end
  // k will be the first position in the right subarray
  int k = partition(array, i-1, j, key(array[j]));
  swap(array[k], array[j]);                // Put pivot in place
  if (k = K) DONE;
  else if (k > K)
    findK(array, i, k-1, K);    // Search in left partition
  else findK(array, k+1, j, K); // Search in right partition
}
```

10.3 Binary search is faster since the self-organizing search cost grows faster. Note, however, that self-organizing search may be faster when the time to sort prior to binary search is an important factor.

10.4 Count: 7 6 4 3 2 0 1 5; the number of searches is 53.

Move-to-front: 6 7 4 2 3 0 1 5; the number of searches is 59.

Transpose: 0 1 3 4 7 6 2 5; the number of searches is 95.

10.5 For count, visit each record in turn in the order that will visit the last element each time. For example, if for the values 0 to 7 stored in ascending order initially, visit them in reverse order (from 7 down to 0).

For Move-to-Front, again visit in reverse order.

For Transpose, alternately visit the last two elements, as described in the book.

```
10.6 void FreqCount(ELEM* array, int* count) {
        // Assume that array is empty to begin with
        int n = 0;
        while ((int val = GETNEXT()) != DONE) {
          for (i=0; i<n; i++)
            if (array[i] == val) break;
          if (i == n) {
            array[n] = val;
            count[n+] = 1;
          }
          else {
            count[i]++;
            while ((i > 0) && (count[i] > count[i-1])) {
              swap(array[i], array[i-1]);
              swap(count[i], count[i-1]);
            }
          }
        }
      }

10.7 void MoveToFront(ELEM* array) {
        // Assume that array is empty to begin with
        int n = 0;
        while ((int val = GETNEXT()) != DONE) {
          for (i=0; i<n; i++)
            if (array[i] == val) break;
          if (i == n) array[n] = val;
          while (i > 0)
            swap(array[i], array[i-1]);
        }
      }

10.8 void tanspose(ELEM* array) {
        // Assume that array is empty to begin with
        int n = 0;
        while ((int val = GETNEXT()) != DONE) {
          for (i=0; i<n; i++)
            if (array[i] == val) break;
          if (i == n) array[n] = val;
          if (i != 0)
            swap(array[i], array[i-1]);
        }
      }
```

10.9
```
// in1 and in2 are input bit vectors, out is output bit vector;
// n is length of bit vector in ints.  Assume the length of the
// bit vectors are always a number of ints.
void union(int* in1, int* in2, int* out, int n) {
  for (int i=0; i<n; i++)
    out[i] = in1[i] | in2[i];
}


// in1 and in2 are input bit vectors, out is output bit vector;
// n is length of bit vector in ints.  Assume the length of the
// bit vectors are alwasy a number of ints.
void inter(int* in1, int* in2, int* out, int n) {
  for (int i=0; i<n; i++)
    out[i] = in1[i] & in2[i];
}


// in1 and in2 are input bit vectors, out is output bit vector;
// n is length of bit vector in ints.  Assume the length of the
// bit vectors are alwasy a number of ints.
void diff(int* in1, int* in2, int* out, int n) {
  for (int i=0; i<n; i++)
    out[i] = in1[i] & ~in2[i];
}
```

10.10 **(a)** The probability p can be computed as follows:

$$p = 1 - \overline{p} = 1 - \frac{364 * 363 * \cdots * 343}{365 * 365 * \cdots * 365} \approx 50.7\%.$$

My simulation program give 50.5%.

(b) My simulation program gives 64.4%

(c) Simplify this problem by assuming that each month has equal probability for having an individual's birthday. Five students is sufficient – in fact, for five students the probability of a match is over 60% My simulation program gives 42.9% for 4 people, and 62.2% for 5 people.

10.11 **(a)** No – if $K \geq n^2$ then the result will be out of the range of the hash table.

(b) Yes –but is the worst possible hash function since all values hash to the same location.

(c) No – it is not possible to recover the location of the element once it is stored using a random number.

(d) Yes – this may be a reasonable hash function, if K tends to be much larger than n.

10.12 The table will store values in order:

```
Slot:  0  1  2  3   4  5  6
Value:       9  3   2  12
```

Slot 0 and 1 will be filled next with probability 1/7. Slot 6 will be filled next with probability 5/7.

10.13 Using a hash table of size 101, here are the results.

(a) 20

(b) 71

(c) 37

10.14 Key: 2 8 31 20 19 18 53 27
H1: 2 8 5 7 6 5 1 1
H2: 3 9 1 1 2 3 1 5
Result of inserting:

$2 \to 2$ OK
$8 \to 8$ OK
$31 \to 5$ OK
$20 \to 7$ OK
$19 \to 6$ OK
$18 \to 5$ Collision. So, try 5+3 = 8. Collision.
    Then 5+6 = 11. OK
$53 \to 1$ OK
$27 \to 1$ Collision. So, try 1+5 = 6. Collision.
    Then 1+5+5 = 11. Collision.
    Then 1+5+5+5 % 13 = 3. OK

Final table:

```
Position:  0   1  2   3  4   5   6   7  8  9  10  11  12
Value:         53  2  27     31  19  20  8          18
```

10.15
```
void hashDelete(ELEM R) {
    int home;                    // Home position for R
    int pos = home = h(key(R)); // Initial pos on probe sequence
    for (int i=1; key(T[pos]) != key(R); i++) {
      pos = (home + p(key(R), i)) % M; // Next slot on sequence
      if (key(T[pos]) == EMPTY) ERROR; // Not in table
    }
    T[pos] = TOMBSTONE;                     // Insert R
}

void hashInsert(ELEM R) {      // Insert record R into table T
    int home;                    // Home position for R
    int pos = home = h(key(R)); // Initial position on sequence
    for (int i=1; ((key(T[pos]) != EMPTY) &&
                   (key(T[pos]) != TOMBSTONE)); i++) {
      pos = (home + p(key(R), i)) % M; // Next slot on sequence
      if (key(T[pos]) == key(R)) ERROR; // Don't allow duplicates
    }
    T[pos] = R;                  // Insert R
}

ELEM hashSearch(KEY K) { // Search for the record with key K
    int home;               // Home position for K
    int pos = home = h(K); // Initial position on probe sequence
    for (int i=1; (key(T[pos])!=K) && (key(T[pos])!=EMPTY); i++)
      pos = (home + p(K, i)) % M;  // Next position on sequence
    if (key(T[pos] == K)) return T[pos];  // Found it
    else return UNSUCCESSFUL;       // K not in hash table
}
```

10.16 This "random" probe sequence yields identical results to using linear probing with a constant skip factor of 2. In other words, if an element has its home slot at position 2, it will follow the same probe sequence as an element whose home slot is at position 0 and probed one time to slot 2. Thus, we must be careful that the random permutation does not have properties of regular behavior as shown by this series.

11

Indexing

11.1 **(a)** Assuming that the linear index stores a key and a 4 byte block number, the index can hold information for 32K blocks, for a total file size of 32MB, or 4M records.

(b) This second level index allows the first level index to be 128 blocks, or 16K records long. Thus, the record file can contain 16K blocks, or 16MB, which is 2M records. While this is smaller than the situation in (a), there is only a very small amount of main memory in use.

11.2 **(a)** Assuming that the linear index stores a key and a 4 byte block number, the index can hold information for 256K blocks. Assume that a block hold $\lfloor 4096/68 \rfloor = 60$ records. Thus, the data file can hold up to 15,728,640 records.

(b) This second level index allows the first level index to be 1024 blocks, or .5M records long. Thus, the record file can contain .5M blocks, which is 30M records.

11.3 No change needs to be made, since the data value itself is not used by the binary search function, only the key which is stored in the index.

11.4 The linear index will store the key values in sorted order, with each key having a pointer to its string.

11.5 (a)

sec key	index	index	primary key
DEER	0	0	2398
DUCK	4	1	3456
FROG	7	2	8133
GOAT	9	3	9737
		4	2936
		5	7183
		6	9279
		7	1111
		8	7186
		9	7739

(b)

sec key	index	index	primary key	Next
DEER	0	0	2398	1
DUCK	4	1	3456	2
FROG	7	2	8133	3
GOAT	9	3	9737	-1
		4	2936	5
		5	7183	6
		6	9279	-1
		7	1111	8
		8	7186	-1
		9	7739	-1

11.6 ISAM is space efficient, more so than the B-tree. If few records are inserted, the ISAM system will work well. ISAM will continue to work well even if a number of records are deleted.

11.7 The 2-3 tree of k levels will have the fewest nodes if no parent has three children. We know from Chapter 5 that the complete binary tree with k levels has at least 2^{k-1} leaves.

The 2-3 tree of k levels will have the most nodes if every parent has three children. A 3-ary tree with k levels can have as many as 3^{k-1} nodes.

11.8

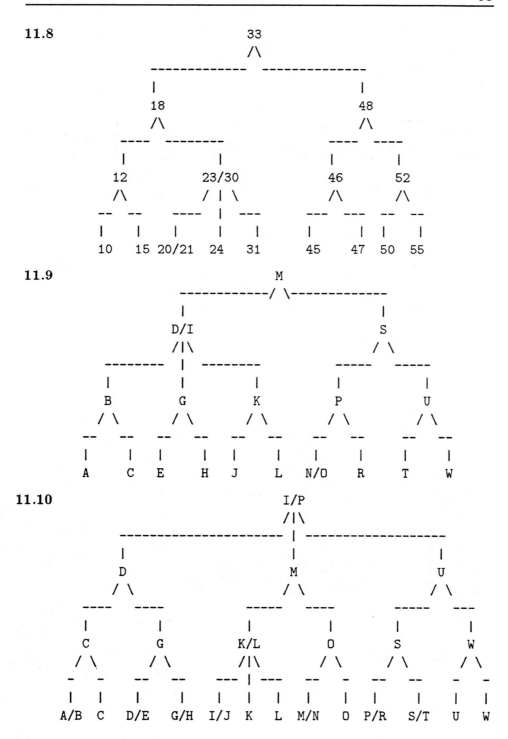

```
                                  33
                                  /\
            ------------     --------------
            |                          |
            18                         48
            /\                         /\
      ----  --------               ----  ----
      |            |               |        |
      12        23/30             46       52
      /\        / | \             /\       /\
    --  --    ----  |  ---      ---  ---  --  --
    |    |    |     |   |       |     |  |    |
    10   15  20/21  24  31      45    47 50   55
```

11.9

```
                              M
            ------------/ \-------------
            |                       |
            D/I                     S
            /|\                    / \
      --------  |  --------     -----  -----
      |         |         |     |        |
      B         G         K     P        U
     / \       / \       / \   / \      / \
    --  --    --  --    --  -- --  --   --  --
    |    |    |    |    |    | |    |   |    |
    A    C    E    H    J    L N/O  R   T    W
```

11.10

```
                              I/P
                              /|\
            --------------------  |  ------------------
            |                     |                  |
            D                     M                  U
           / \                   / \                / \
        ----  ----            -----  ----        -----  ---
        |        |            |        |         |        |
        C        G           K/L       O         S        W
       / \      / \          /|\      / \       / \      / \
      -   -    --  --      ---  |  --- --  -    --  --   -   -
      |   |    |    |      |    |   |  |    |   |    |   |   |
     A/B  C   D/E  G/H    I/J   K   L  M/N  O  P/R  S/T  U   W
```

11.11
```
                    24/48
                    / | \
            ------- | -----------
            |       |           |
          same    33/45         55
                  / | \         /\
                --- | ---      -- --
                |   |   |      |   |
              30/31 38  47   50/52 60
```

11.12
```
                                  18/33
                                  / | \
        -------------------------- | -----------
        |                          |           |
      4/10                        23          same
      / | \                       /\
    ----- | ------           ------- ---
    |     |      |           |         |
  1/2/3 4/5/6  10/12/15   18/19/20/21/22  23/30/31
```

11.13
```
                 23/33
                 / | \
          ---------- | ----------
          |         |          |
  10/12/15/21/22  23/30/31  45/47/48/50/52
```

11.14
```
        -------------------- GMS --------------------
        |                     | |                  |
        |            |-------| |--------|          |
        |            |                 |           |
      -- D --    --- IK ---        --- P ---    ---- U ----
      |     |    |   |   |         |       |  |         |
      |     |    |   |   |         |       |  |         |
     ABC   DE   GH  IJ   K        MNO     PR ST        UW
```

11.15

	min	max
1	0	15
2	16	1500
3	800	150,000
4	40,000	15,000,000
5	2,000,000	1,500,000,000

11.16

	min	max
1	0	50
2	50	2500
3	1250	125,000
4	31,250	6,250,000
5	781,250	312,500,000

12

Lists and Arrays Revisited

12.1 Here is the final Skip List.

```
head       2     5     20    25    26    30    31

+------->  +-->  +-->  +-->  +-->  +-->  +-->  /

+----------->  +-------->  +-->  /

+----------->  +------------>  /

+--------------------------->  /
```

12.2 For each even numbered node i, i can be written as $j2^k$ for the largest possible integer k. For example, 8 is $1 * 2^3$ and 12 is $3 * 2^2$. Each even numbered node $j2^k$ stores a pointer to $(j+1)2^k$. This makes access time $2 \log n + 1$ in the worst case. Odd numbered nodes i can point to node $i + 2$ to speed the search somewhat.

12.3 The average number of pointers for a Skip List with n nodes is $2n$ (not counting the header).

12.4
```
ELEM SkipList::remove(ELEM Value) { // Remove from Skip List
    SkipNode *x = head;          // Start at header node
    SkipNode* update[level];     // Update tracks end of each level
    // Search for  element prior to Value
    for(int i=level; i>=0; i--) {
        while((x->forward[i] != NULL) &&
              (key(x->forward[i]->value) < key(Value)))
            x = x->forward[i];
        update[i] = x;           // Keep track of end at level i
```

68

```
  }
  if (key(x->forward[0]->value) != key(Value))
    return;                    // Value not in list
  x = forward[0];              // Now pointing at node to delete
  for (i=0; i<=x->level; i++) // Fix up the pointers
    update[i]->forward[i] = x->forward[i];
  ELEM temp = x->value;
  delete x;
  return temp;
}
```

12.5 This is something of a trick question. There is no good access method for finding the ith node, other than to count over i pointers at level 0.

```
*SkipNode SkipList::ithnode(int i) {
  *SkipNode curr = head;
  for(int j=0; j<i; j++) {
    if (curr->forward[0] == NULL)
      return NULL;  // No ith node in list
    curr = curr->forward[0];
  }
  return curr;
}
```

12.6 A regular array cell requires 8 bytes (a value. A sparse matrix cell requires 4 pointers, two indices and a value for a total of 28 bytes. If the array contains more than 8/28 or 29% non-zero-valued elements, then the regular array representation will be more space efficient. Note that this ignores the space required for the row and column headers, which will be $10(M + N)$ for and $M \times N$ matrix.

12.7
```
\\ Written so that tail returns the tail of the list
MLnode* reverse(MLnode* rt) {
    if (rt == NULL) return NULL;
    rt->child = reverse(rt->child);
    if (rt->next == NULL) return rt; // Only element on list
    MLnode* newrt = reverse(rt->next);
    rt->next->next = rt; // rt->next still points at original
                         // next node
                         // (which is now tail of reversed list)
    rt->next = NULL;
    return newrt;
}
```

```
12.8 void SparseMatrix insert(int r, int c, int val) {
       for (SMhead* crow = row;
            (crow->index <= r) && (crow->next != NULL);
            crow = crow->next);  // First, find the row
       if (crow->index != r) // Make a new row
         crow->next = new SMhead(r, crow->next, NULL);
       for (SMhead* ccol = col;
            (ccol->index <= c) && (ccol->next != NULL);
            ccol = ccol->next);   // Now, find the column
       if (ccol->index != c) // Make a new row
         ccol->next = new SMhead(c, ccol->next, NULL);
       // Now, put in its row;
       if ((crow->first == NULL) || (crow->first->col > c))
         SMElem* temp = crow->first =
                     new SMElem(val, crow->first, NULL, NULL, NULL);
       else {
         for (SMElem* temp = crow->first;
              (temp->col <= col) && (temp->nextcol != NULL);
              temp = temp->nextcol);
         if (temp->col == c) { // Replace entry value
           temp->value = val;
           return;
         }
         temp->nextcol =
           new SMElem(val, temp->nextcol, temp, NULL, NULL);
         temp = temp->nextcol;
         temp->nextcol->prevcol = temp;
       }
       // Finally, put in its column;
       if ((ccol->first == NULL) || (ccol->first->row > c)) {
         temp->nextrow = ccol->first;
         temp->prevcol = NULL;
         ccol->first = temp;
       }
       else {
         for (SMElem* tempc = ccol->first; (tempc->row <= row) &&
              (tempc->nextrow != NULL); tempc = tempc->nextrow);
         temp->prevrow = tempc;
         temp->nextrow = tempc->nextrow;
         tempc->nextrow->prevrow = temp;
         tempc->nextrow = temp;
       }
     }
```

```
12.9 void SparseMatrix remove(int r, int c) {
       // First, find the row
       for (SMhead* crow = row;
            (crow->index <= r) && (crow->next != NULL);
            crow = crow->next);
       if (crow->index != r) ERROR;  // Not in array
       // Now, find the column
       for (SMhead* ccol = c;
            (ccol->index <= c) && (ccol->next != NULL);
            ccol = ccol >next);
       if (ccol->index != c) ERROR;  // Not in array
       // Now, find the element
       for (SMElem* temp = crow->first;
            (temp != NULL) && (temp->col != c);
            temp = temp->nextcol);
       if (temp->col != c) ERROR;  // Not in array
       // Now, detatch the element
       if (temp->prevrow == NULL) {
         ccol->first = temp->nextrow;
         if (temp->nextrow != NULL)
           temp->nextrow->prevrow = NULL;
       }
       else {
         temp->prevrow->nextrow = temp->nextrow;
         if (temp->nextrow != NULL)
           temp->nextrow->prevrow = temp->prevrow;
       }
       if (temp->prevcol == NULL) {
         crow->first = temp->nextcol;
         if (temp->nextcol != NULL)
           temp->nextcol->prevcol = NULL;
       }
       else {
         temp->prevcol->nextcol = temp->nextcol;
         if (temp->nextcol != NULL)
           temp->nextcol->prevcol = temp->prevcol;
       }
     }
```

12.10 Transposing a sparse matrix is fairly straightforward. Here is pseudocode:

```
void SparseMatrix::transpose() {
  // For each element, switch its row and column pointers,
  // and its row/column indices.
  for (each row)
    for (each element in the row) {
      swap(nextrow, nextcol);
      swap(prevrow, prevcol);
      swap(row, col);
    }
  swap(row, col); // Swap the row and column list headers
}
```

12.11 Here is pseudocode to add two sparse matrices.

```
void SparseMatrix::add(SparseMatrix& In1, SparseMatrix& In2) {
  // The current object will be the result of adding its
  // two inputs.
  SMhead *temp1 = In1->row;
  SMhead *temp2 = In2->row;

  while ((temp1 != NULL) || (temp2 != NULL))
    if ((temp2 == NULL) || (temp1->index < temp2->index)) {
      // Insert row from first matrix
      for (each elem in temp1's row)
        this.insert(elem->value, elem->row, elem->col);
    }
    else if ((temp1==NULL) || (temp2->index < temp1->index)) {
      // Insert row from second matrix
      for (each elem in temp2's row)
        this.insert(elem->value, elem->row, elem->col);
    }
    else { // Both matrices have this row
      SMElem* curr1 = temp1->first;
      SMElem* curr2 = temp2->first;
      if ((curr2 == NULL) || (curr1->col < curr2->col)) {
        // Insert element from first matrix
        this.insert(curr1->value, curr1->row, curr1->col);
        curr1 = curr1->nextcol;
      }
      else if ((curr1 == NULL) || (curr2->col < curr1->col)) {
        // Insert element from second matrix
        this.insert(curr2->value, curr2->row, curr2->col);
```

```
        curr2 = curr2->nextcol;
      }
      else { // This element in both matrices
        this.insert(curr1->value + curr2->value,
                    curr2->row, curr2->col);
        curr1 = curr1->nextcol;
        curr2 = curr2->nextcol;
      }
    }
  }
```

12.12 This is quite simple. The memory pool is simply viewed as a stack. Requests pop off the requested amount of storage (move the top pointer down). Returns push the storage back on the stack (move the top pointer up). Just re-implement the stack functions for variable length records.

12.13 Simply manage the memory pool as an array-based queue, with variable length records. Memory requests move the rear pointer by the appropriate amount; memory returns move the front pointer by the appropriate amount.

12.14 Here is pseudocode for the release routine. To complete, simply instantiate the appropriate fields as indicated in allocate code on Page 380.

```
void release(int* block) {
  if (the adjacent following block is free) {
    Adjust size of current block;
    Copy following block's list pointers to current block;
    if (the previous block is free) {
      Adjust the size field of the previous block;
      Remove current block from the freelist;
    }
  }
  else if (the previous block is free)
    Adjust the size field of the previous block;
  else { // No merging, need to splice block into linked list
    Append current block to the freelist;
  }
}
```

12.15 **(a)** 1300, 2000, 1000

(b) 1000, 2000, 1300

(c) 900, 1300, 1100, 1000

13

Advanced Tree Structures

13.1

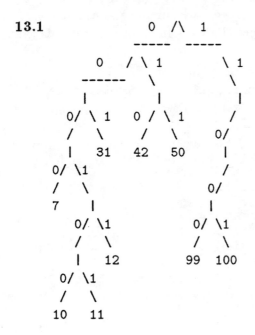

13.2

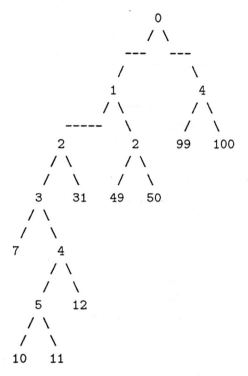

13.3 Binary Trie insertion routine. Assume that the Trie class has a root pointer named "root" and a member named "level" to tell how many bits are in the key.

```
void Trie::insert(int value) {
  TrieNode* temp = root;
  int currlev = level;
  if (root == NULL)
    root = new TrieNode(value);
  else
    while (TRUE) {
      if (temp->isLeaf()) { // Push down existing value
        int tempval = temp->value;
        if (bit(tempval, level) == 1)
          temp->right = new TrieNode(tempvalue);
        else
          temp->left = new TrieNode(tempvalue);
      }
      if (bit(value, currlev) == 1)
        if (temp->right == NULL) {
          temp->right = new TrieNode(value);
```

```
          return;
        }
        else {
          temp = temp->right;
          currlev--;
        }
      else
        if (temp->left == NULL) {
          temp->left = new TrieNode(value);
          return;
        }
        else {
          temp = temp->left;
          currlev--;
        }
    }
}
```

13.4
```
void Trie::removehelp(TrieNode*& rt, int val, int level) {
    if (rt == NULL) cout << val << " is not in the tree.\n";
    else if (rt->value == val) {
      TrieNode* temp = rt;
      rt == NULL
      delete temp;
    }
    else if (bit(val, level) == 0)    // Check left
      removehelp(rt->left, val, level);
    else                              // Check right
      removehelp(rt->right, val);
    // Now, collapse a  node with a single leaf child
    if ((rt->left == NULL) && (rt->right->value != EMPTY)) {
      rt->value = rt->right->value;
      delete rt->right;
      rt->right = NULL;
    }
    if ((rt->right == NULL) && (rt->left->value != EMPTY)) {
      rt->value = rt->left->value;
      delete rt->left
      rt->left = NULL;
    }
}
```

13.5
```
        75
       /  \
     17    89
       \     \
        72    90
       /        \
      25          99
     /  \
   18   42
```

13.6
```
        18
       /  \
     17    89
          /  \
        25    90
          \     \
           72    99
          /  \
        42   75
```

13.7
```
   A(20, 90)
       \
        \
         B(95, 85)
        /
       /
   C(98, 35)
       \
        \
         D(117, 52)
        /
       /
   E(110, 25)
```

13.8   0   127
```
        --------------------
      0|          | C  |    |
       |          |    |    |
       |    A     |----+----|
       |          | D  |    |
       |          |    |    |
       |---------+---------|
       | B  | E  |         |
       |    |    |         |
       |----+----|    F    |
       |    |    |         |
       |    |    |         |
        --------------------
```

13.9 // Return TRUE iff rectangle R intersects circle with
        // centerpoint C and radius Rad.
        boolean Check_Intersect(Rectangle* R, Point* C, double Rad)
        {
        double Rad2;

        Rad2 = Rad * Rad;
        // Translate coordinates, placing C at the origin
        R->max.x -= C->x;   R->max.y -= C->y;
        R->min.x -= C->x;   R->min.y -= C->y;

        if (R->max.x < 0) // R to left of circle center
          if (R->max.y < 0) // R in lower left corner
            return (R->max.x * R->max.x + R->max.y * R->max.y) < Rad2;
          else if (R->min.y > 0) // R in upper left corner
            return (R->max.x * R->max.x + R->min.y * R->min.y) < Rad2;
          else // R due West of circle
            return ABS(R->max.x) < Rad;
        else if (R->min.x > 0) // R to right of circle center
          if (R->max.y < 0) // R in lower right corner
            return (R->min.x * R->min.x) < Rad2;
          else if (R->min.y > 0) // R in upper right corner
            return (R->min.x * R->min.x + R->min.y + R->min.y) < Rad2;
          else // R due East of circle
            return R->min.x < Rad;
        else // R on circle vertical centerline
          if (R->max.y < 0) // R due South of circle
            return ABS(R->max.y) < Rad;

```
        else if (R->min.y > 0)   // R due North of circle
          return R->min.y < Rad;
        else // R contains circle centerpoint
          return TRUE;
      }
```

13.10
```
        /\
       /  \
      A   /\
         /  \
        /\   B
       /  \
         /\
        /  \
      E   /\
         /  \
        C    D
```

13.11
```
              A
      -----------------------
      |   |   |           |
          C   B           D
                    -------------
                    |  |   |   |
                       E       F
```

14

Analysis Techniques

14.1 Guess that the solution is of the form

$$an^3 + bn^2 + cn + d.$$

Since when $n = 0$ the summation is 0, we know that $d = 0$. We have the following simultaneous equations available:

$$
\begin{aligned}
a + b + c &= 1 \\
8a + 4b + 2c &= 5 \\
27a + 9b + 3c &= 14
\end{aligned}
$$

Solving this set, we get $a = 1/3$, $b = 1/2$ and $c = 1/6$, yielding Equation 2.2.

14.2 Guess that the solution is of the form

$$an^4 + bn^3 + cn^2 + dn + e.$$

Since when $n = 0$ the summation is 0, we know that $e = 0$. We have the following simultaneous equations available:

$$
\begin{aligned}
a + b + c + d &= 1 \\
16a + 8b + 4c + 2d &= 9 \\
81a + 27b + 9c + 3d &= 36 \\
256a + 64b + 16c + 4d &= 100
\end{aligned}
$$

Solving this set, we get $a = 1/4$, $b = 1/2$, $c = 1/4$, and $d = 0$. Thus, the closed form formula is

$$\frac{n^4 + 2n^3 + n^2}{4}.$$

The student should verify by induction.

14.3 From Equation 2.2 we know that

$$\sum_{i=1}^{n} i^2 = \frac{2n^3 + 3n^2 + n}{6}.$$

Thus, when summing the range $a \le i \le b$, we get

$$\sum_{i=a}^{b} i^2 = \frac{2b^3 + 3b^2 + b}{6} - \frac{2a^3 + 3a^2 + a}{6}$$

$$= \frac{2(b^3 - a^3) + 3(b^2 - a^2) + (b - a)}{6}.$$

14.4 We need to do some rearranging of the summation to get something to work with. Start with

$$\sum_{i=1}^{n} i^2 = \sum_{i=1}^{n} (i + 1 - 1)^2.$$

Substituting i for $i - 1$, we get

$$\sum_{i=1}^{n} i^2 = \sum_{i=0}^{n-1} (i + 1)^2$$

$$= \sum_{i=0}^{n-1} (i^2 + 2i + 1).$$

The i^2 terms mostly cancel, leaving

$$n^2 = \sum_{i=0}^{n-1} (2i + 1)$$

$$= 2\sum_{i=0}^{n-1} i + n.$$

$$\frac{n^2 - n}{2} = \sum_{i=0}^{n-1} i$$

Substituting back $i - 1$ for i, we get

$$\sum_{i=1}^{n} = \frac{n^2 + n}{2}.$$

14.5

$$F(n) = 2 + 4 + \cdots + 2^n$$
$$2F(n) = 4 + 8 + \cdots + 2^{n+1}$$

When we subtract, we get $2F(n) - F(n) = F(n) = 2^{n+1} - 2$. Thus,

$$\sum_{i=1}^{n} 2^i = 2^{n+1} - 2.$$

14.6 Call our summation $G(n)$, then

$$G(n) = \sum_{i=1}^{n} i2^{n-i} = 2^{n-1} + 2 * 2^{n-2} + 3 * 2^{n-3} + \cdots + n * 2^0.$$

$$2G(n) = 2\sum_{i=1}^{n} i2^{n-i} = 2^n + 2 * 2^{n-1} + 3 * 2^{n-2} + \cdots + n * 2^1.$$

Subtracting, we get

$$2G(n) - G(n) = G(n) = 2^n + 2^{n-1} + 2^{n-2} + \cdots + 2^1 - n * 2^0.$$

This is simply $2^{n+1} - 2 - n$.

14.7 TOH has recurrence relation $F(n) = 2F(n-1) + 1, F(1) = 1$. Since the problem gives us the closed form solution, we can easily prove it by induction.

14.8 The closed form solution is $F(n) = nc$, which can easily be proved using induction.

14.9 Pick the constants $c = 1, n_0 = 4$, prove for powers of 2.

Base Case: For $n = 4, F(n) = n + 2 > 2\log 2$. Thus, the theorem holds.

Induction Hypothesis: For $n \leq k$, $F(n) > k\log k$.

Induction Step: $F(2k) = 2F(k) + 2k$. By the induction hypothesis, we get $F(2k) = 2F(k) + n > 2(k\log k) + 2k = 2k\log k + 2k$. Now, $2k\log 2k = 2k(\log k + 1) = 2k\log k + 2$, which is clearly less than $2k\log k + 2k$. Thus, the theorem holds by the principle of Mathematical Induction.

14.10 Expanding the recurrence, we get

$$\sqrt{n} + \sqrt{n/2} + \sqrt{n/4} + \cdots + 1.$$

Clearly this is smaller than $\sqrt{n}\log n$, so we will guess that $\mathbf{T}(n) = \Theta(\sqrt{n}\log n$. To complete the proof we would need to show that $\mathbf{T}(n)$ is in $\Omega(\sqrt{n}\log n)$, but this turns out to be impossible.

On the other hand, the recurrence is clearly $\Omega\sqrt{n}$. So, let's guess that $\mathbf{T}(n)$ is in $O(\sqrt{n})$ for $c = 4, n_0 = 2$. We prove this by induction.

Base case: $\mathbf{T}(2) = 1 + \sqrt{2} < 4\sqrt{2}$, so the hypothesis is correct.

Induction Hypothesis: For any value less than or equal to k, $\mathbf{T}(k) < 4\sqrt{k}$.

Induction Step: For $2k$,

$$\mathbf{T}(2k) = \mathbf{T}(k) + \sqrt{2k}.$$

By the induction hypothesis,

$$\mathbf{T}(k) + \sqrt{2k} < 4\sqrt{k} + \sqrt{2k}.$$

For the theorem to be correct,

$$\mathbf{T}(k) + \sqrt{2k} < 4\sqrt{k} + \sqrt{2k} < 4\sqrt{2k}$$

which is true. Thus, by the principle of Mathematical Induction, the theorem is correct.

14.11 Expanding the recurrence, we get

$$\begin{aligned}
\mathbf{T}(n) &= 2\mathbf{T}(n/2) + n \\
&= 2(2\mathbf{T}(n/4) + n/2) + n \\
&= 2(2(2\mathbf{T}(n/8) + n/4) + n/2) + n \\
&= 2(2(\cdots 2(2 + 4) + 8) + \cdots) + n \\
&= \sum_{i=1}^{\log n} 2^i 2^{\log n - i} \\
&= n\log n.
\end{aligned}$$

14.12 For binary search, $\mathbf{T}(n) = \mathbf{T}(n/2) + 1$. By Theorem 14.1, $1 = 2^0$, so the recurrence is $\Theta(n^0 \log n) = \Theta(\log n)$.

14.13 Assume that the hash table is originally of size 2B. Once insert B elements, we must reinsert them again. Once we have inserted another B elements, 2B elements are reinserted, then after another 2B get inserted, 4B get reinserted. Thus, the first B elements inserted are repeatedly reinserted, the next B elements are repeatedly reinserted one fewer times, the next 2B elements 2 fewer times, etc. Thus, once we insert $2^i B$ elements, we have done a total number of insertions costing $2^i B + 2^{i-1} B + 2^{i-2} 2B + \cdots + 2^{i-1} B$. This works out to requiring about two inserts per element.

14.14 **(a)** By adding the components in each quadrant of the matrix, you will find that

$$
\begin{aligned}
s_1 + s_2 - s_4 + s_6 &= A_{11} B_{11} + A_{12} B_{21} \\
s_4 + s_5 &= A_{11} B_{12} + A_{12} B_{22} \\
s_6 + s_7 &= A_{21} B_{11} + A_{22} B_{21} \\
s_2 - s_3 + s_5 - s_7 &= A_{21} B_{12} + A_{22} B_{22}
\end{aligned}
$$

(b) Strassen's algorithm requires 7 matrix multiplies and 18 matrix additions, while the regular algorithm requires 8 matrix multiplies and 4 matrix additions. The recurrence relation for Strassen's algorithm is

$$ T(n) = 7T(n/2) + 18(n/2)^2 $$

while the recurrence relation for the regular algorithm is

$$ T(n) = 8T(n/2) + 4(n/2)^2 $$

(c) Plugging the constants from the recurrence relation into Theorem 14.1, we find that Strassen's algorithm is $\Theta(n^{\log_2 7}) \approx \Theta(n^{2.81})$. The regular algorithm is $\Theta(n^3)$.

(d) While Strassen's algorithm gives a theoretical speedup, the constant is very large. Thus, it requires impractical sizes of n for Strassen's algorithm to be faster than the regular algorithm.

14.15 First, note that we are clearly discussing an upper bound here. In the case of large N and small M, there might be no node splits at all. The bound is also achievable, since a packed tree with each leaf node receiving an insert would cause every node to split. The question is, how bad can things get?

Given a tree of N nodes, with every node full, there is a potential for N node splits with no nodes being inserted "for free." Each node split creates two nodes each with an open space, thus lowering the potential of the tree by one for each node split. Each insertion of an element into a node that is not-yet-full raises the potential by one. Thus, the amortized cost for M inserts is at most $M + N$ node splits.

14.16 (a) The amortized cost is 2 inserts/element since we can get growth by n positions only after inserting n elements.

   (b) Fill an array with $2^n + 1$ elements, which forces a final growth to an array of size 2^{n+1}. Now, do an arbitrarily long series of alternating inserts and deletes. This will cause the array to repeatedly shrink and grow, for bad ($\Theta(n^2)$) performance.

   (c) If we shrink the array whenever the space use goes below 25%, we will have the desired performance.

14.17 Each node can be visited only once. Thus, there is initially potential for $|V|$ node visits. We can look at each edge only once (the edges out of a node are visited when the node is visited). Thus, there is potential for $|E|$ edge visits. The initial call to DFS can expend a small part of that potential, or a large part. But, the sum of all the calls to DFS must cost $\Theta(|V| + |E|)$.

14.18 As with Move-to-Front, the contribution of unsuccessful searches requiring comparisons between keys A and B is independent of other keys. We have an unsuccessful search for A if and only if we have had more requests for B so far. Assuming that B is requested R_B times and A is requested R_A times with $R_B > R_A$, we can only have unsuccessful searches twice the number of times that A is requested. This happens at most for R_A requests to B occurring before R_A requests to A. The remaining requests to B are successful without encountering A. Thus, the Count heuristic can have cost at most twice that of the optimal static ordering.

15

Limits to Computation

15.1 This reduction provides an upper bound of $O(n \log n)$ for the problem of maximum finding (that is the time for the entire process), and a lower bound of constant time for SORTING (since that is the time spent by Maximum Finding in this process). Neither bound is particularly enlightening. There is no true reduction from SORTING to Maximum Finding (in the sense that the transformations do not dominate the cost) since SORTING is an intrinsicly more difficult problem than Maximum Finding.

15.2 Consider the following fact:

$$\begin{bmatrix} A & B \\ 0 & 0 \end{bmatrix}^2 = \begin{bmatrix} A^2 & AB \\ 0 & 0 \end{bmatrix}.$$

Thus, if we had an algorithm that could square an $n \times n$ matrix in less time than needed to multiply two matrices, we could use a transformation based on this fact to speed up matrix multiplication.

15.3 Consider the following fact:

$$\begin{bmatrix} 0 & A & 0 \\ 0 & 0 & 0 \\ 0 & 0 & 0 \end{bmatrix} \begin{bmatrix} 0 & 0 & 0 \\ 0 & 0 & B \\ 0 & 0 & 0 \end{bmatrix} = \begin{bmatrix} 0 & 0 & AB \\ 0 & 0 & 0 \\ 0 & 0 & 0 \end{bmatrix}.$$

Thus, if we had an algorithm that could multiply two $n \times n$ upper triangular matrices in less time than needed to multiply two matrices, we could use a transformation based on this fact to speed up matrix multiplication.

15.4 **(a)** The input (the number n) require $\log n$ bits to represent it. However, n multiplication operations are required. Thus, the work is exponential on the input size.

   (b) It is possible to compute x^n in $\log n$ time, and the rest of the formula requires a constant number of multiplications. Thus, the number of multiplications required is polynomial on the input size.

15.5 First, we should note that, for both problems, the decision problem is being considered.

TRAVELING SALESMAN is $\mathcal{NP}$-complete if (1) it is in $\mathcal{NP}$, and (2) it is $\mathcal{NP}$-hard. Proving (1) is easy, just provide a non-deterministic polynomial time algorithm. To prove (2), we will reduce to TRAVELING SALESMAN from the known $\mathcal{NP}$-complete problem HAMILTONIAN CYCLE. First, we transform an input to HAMILTONIAN CYCLE into an input to TRAVELING SALESMAN by giving each edge of the input graph an arbitrary distance of 1, and then picking any arbitrary (large) number for the total distance to beat. Then if TRAVELING SALESMAN returns "YES", we know that there exists a Hamiltonian cycle in the graph since a salesman's circuit is a Hamiltonian cycle. If TRAVELING SALESMAN returns "NO" then no such cycle exists.

15.6 To prove that K-CLIQUE is $\mathcal{NP}$-complete, prove that it is in $\mathcal{NP}$ and that it is $\mathcal{NP}$-hard. Clearly it is in $\mathcal{NP}$ since a nondeterministic algorithm is simply to guess a set of vertices of size K to form the clique, and check in polynomial time that the guess is correct.

To prove that K-CLIQUE is $\mathcal{NP}$-hard, use a reduction from the known $\mathcal{NP}$-complete problem, VERTEX COVER. The necessary insight is that, given a graph of n vertices with a K-clique, the inverse graph has a Vertex Cover of size $n - K$. (The inverse graph G' of G has an edge between two vertices if and only if G does not.) Clearly this transformation is correct, because the nodes making up the K-Clique in G must have no connecting edges in G', so selecting the other $n - K$ edges for the cover is satisfactory.

Thus, given as input to VERTEX COVER a graph and a size I to beat, the input to K-CLIQUE is the inverse graph and $n - I$ as the size of the Clique.

15.7 The answer to this question is similar to that for Exercise 15.7, since the transformation works in both directions.

15.8 Represent a real number in a bin as an infinite column of binary digits, similar to the representation of functions in Figure 15.4. Now we can use a simple diagonalization proof. Assume that some assignment of real numbers to integers is proposed. We can construct a new real number that has not been assigned by taking the first bit of the number assigned to "1" and flipping it; take the second bit of the number assigned to "2" and flip it; and so on.

15.9 Clearly, KNAPSACK is in $\mathcal{NP}$, since we can just guess a set of items and test in polynomial time if its size is less than k and its value greater than v.

To prove that KNAPSACK is $\mathcal{NP}$-hard, we reduce from the known $\mathcal{NP}$-complete problem EXACT KNAPSACK. EXACT KNAPSACK takes as input some items with sizes and a value k. To convert this input to an input for KNAPSACK, we give each item a value equal to its size. We set $v = k$. We now give this input to KNAPSACK.

If KNAPSACK returns "NO" then there is no solution for EXACT KNAPSACK. If KNAPSACK returns "YES" then the items whose values sum to v must also have size exactly k. Thus, if KNAPSACK returns "YES" then the answer for EXACT KNAPSACK is "YES."

15.10 Take an arbitrary program, and modify it to remove all print statements. Then, at all places where the program might terminate, insert a print statement. This revised program prints if and only if the original program halts. Thus, if we had a program that determined if an arbitrary program prints something, we could use it to solve the HALTING problem.

15.11 Take an arbitrary program, and modify it so that at all places where it might terminate, it makes a call to a new subroutine that contains one empty statement S, then returns. Thus, the original program halts if and only if the new program executes statement S. Thus, if we had a program that determined if an arbitrary program executes a specified statement, we could use it to solve the HALTING problem.

15.12 Fix one input program to be the program that halts if and only if its input is the empty string. Call this program E. Now, take an arbitrary program P and modify it so that it goes into an infinite loop if its input is not empty. call this modified program P'. Now, this modified program halts on empty input if and only if the original program halts on empty input. We can now feed E and P' to our proposed program that determines if two programs halt on the same set of inputs. We now have a solution to the problem of determining if a program halts on the empty input, which we know from the text to be unsolvable.

15.13 See the answer to Exercise 5.12. The modified program halts, if it halts, only for the empty input, so it serves as a solution to this problem as well.